GLOBAL INTERFACE DESIGN

LIMITED WARRANTY AND DISCLAIMER OF LIABILITY

GLOBAL INTERFACE DESIGN
TONY FERNANDES

AP PROFESSIONAL

Boston   San Diego   New York
London   Sydney   Tokyo   Toronto

This book is printed on acid-free paper. ∞

AP PROFESSIONAL
1300 Boylston Street, Chestnut Hill, MA 02167

An Imprint of ACADEMIC PRESS, INC.
A Division of HARCOURT BRACE & COMPANY

United Kingdom Edition published by
ACADEMIC PRESS LIMITED
24–28 Oval Road, London NW1 7DX

Library of Congress Cataloging-in-Publication Data

Fernandes, Tony.
    Global Interface Design / Tony Fernandes.
            p.   cm.
    Includes bibliographical references and index.
    ISBN 0-12-253790-4 (pbk.)—ISBN 0-12-253791-2 (CD-ROM)
    1. User interfaces (Computer systems)   2. Human-computer interaction.   I. Title.
QA76.9.U83F47   1995
306.4—dc20   95-10183
                                                                              CIP

Printed in the United States of America
95 96 97 98   IP   9 8 7 6 5 4 3 2 1

CONTENTS

To my parents Frank and Amelia without whose vision my voyage through countries and cultures would have never begun and to my wife Kathy whose love and support inspired me to create this book.

Preface

To sit down and write a document of any length, you have to feel that you have something to say. In the case of interface design and the world at large, I wanted to say a great deal.

My first recognition of cultural differences came when I was seven. It was at that age that my parents emigrated to the United States from Portugal. The cultural misunderstandings that I witnessed came in many forms. Because we moved in December, many doors in the US were decorated with wreaths to celebrate the holidays. The wreath in Portugal, however, was used to indicate that somebody in the house had died. This was an all too common sight in the 1960s because Portugal was in the midst of vicious war in Angola and Mozambique. You can imagine what my parents must have felt when they drove down the street and saw wreath after wreath during the Vietnam War era United States.

Other forms of misunderstanding came from the similarity of words. For example, *livraria* in Portuguese is similar to library in English. The Portuguese word refers to a book store: there is another word for public library. Of course, figuring out in a foreign language that all those books were not for sale was no easy feat. The Portuguese word for "the common cold" is *constipação,* which is very similar to the English word constipation. When a Portuguese immigrant went to the pharmacy for cold medication, they were often sold a laxative because of this confusion. Yes, it's funny now, but waiting out a cold in the bathroom is not the most pleasant experience.

Having worked in the user interface field for about a decade, it became apparent to me that some of the misunderstandings I experienced as a child were perpetuated by the user interface designs I saw in American products. It was clear to me that many designs would not be understood outside the borders of the US. With this realization, I combined my past experience and my knowledge of user interfaces to create a book that could at least start the dialog about this topic. It was an enormously exciting proposition. The only problem was the amount of material. It became clear early on in the process that all of anthropology, history, and art could be folded in this book. The discussion of any one country could fill an encyclopedia. I made the decision, therefore, to teach people how to think about the problem rather than presenting a list of items to check off for each country. The list approach just doesn't work for issues as large and as complex as culture.

The computer is slowly but surely becoming ubiquitous. It is reaching out to people all over the world as desktop machines, palmtop computers, and through the Worldwide Web. One of my chief concerns regarding software today, particularly American software, is that it is enforcing a new kind of imperialism. Many companies, and many designers in those companies, treat other cultures as inconveniences that cost money to deal with and, as a result, the differences in people are ignored. The expectation is that people will bend and change to use the software the way Americans do. No real thought is put into the taboos and customs with which products can be incompatible. Who gave designers the right to roll over other people's cultures and ignore them? In the past this happened by conquest. North and South America are monuments to the European attitude of several hundred years ago. Then it was religion and land. What is the motive in the information age; greed? What is the excuse: ignorance? There is no excuse. If products are being produced for worldwide consumption, it is a designer's ethical responsibility to understand what that entails. American culture is spreading even further, fueled by the need to use computers. As a reader of this book, think carefully about your motives and your place in the history of the information age. It will be a sad day when you get on a plane, fly 6000 miles and arrive in a place that looks identical to the one you left.

When I put all of this material together, it was clear that it had an American focus. The base examples are all American, followed by departures from the American norm. This focus can be viewed in two ways however. The first is that the structure will be very useful to people overseas who want to understand the US better. The second is that the examples will help Americans understand their own culture and the differences found in other countries. One must understand his or her own culture before he or she can hope to understand somebody else's. The American focus also seemed natural because Americans are wonderfully kind people but they are also generally ignorant of cultures in other parts of the world. What most people know of other countries is what they see on TV. A book can't compete with TV but it can use photographs. This book and companion CD, therefore, are full of glimpses into the seemingly infinite variety of the human condition.

The above describes what the book is, but just as important is what the book is *not*. It is not an academic discussion about existing theories and research in this area. The world is full of user interface books that deal with the problem from a theoretical perspective: I didn't need to add one more to the list. This book concentrates on real issues that real products will encounter in the international marketplace. I also strived to use simple, common English to explain my thoughts. I hate needless jargon.

Although I believe that software should be localized because it is the right thing to do, there are also market reasons to do so. A lack of understanding about other parts of the world can severely effect the usability of a product. My hope is that when you put this book down, you will think about this issue in a slightly different way.

As with any endeavor, there are lots of people behind the scenes that made it possible. I would like to give a special thanks to Lynn Shade of Apple Computer, as well as Shannon Halgren, and German Bauer of Claris Corporation for their help with the content of this book. In addition I would like to thank the following people:

Bill Champ of Claris
Kyoko Desiderio of CCIC
Lisa Burke of Lotus Development Corporation
Kathy Fernandes of Pedra Design
Mary Beth Butler of Lotus Development Corporation
Paul Fernandes of Haemonetics
Studio Japan

If you find a mistake, have a relevant story, or just want to say hello, send me some email at GLOBEUI@AOL.COM. Enjoy the book.

Tony Fernandes

Introduction

People are different: They dress differently, behave differently, and perform different jobs (ii-1). This is true in your neighborhood, in your city, and even in your family. As one travels around the world, these differences become more and more pronounced.

Figure ii-1 Different people

Photographs copyright© 1995 by Tony Fernandes

User interface design is about these very same people. It is a user interface designer's goal is to create an experience that is easy for the user to understand and a tool that is easy to use. To accomplish this, designers draw upon the real world in order to empower users with the knowledge they already have. This approach works beautifully but there's one problem: The real world varies from country to country and continent to continent. The designer's world and their user's world become very different. If these differences go unnoticed, biases can creep into the design. Biases that can severely effect the usability of a user interface.

National biases are borne out of several sources of information. Pop culture is certainly one. Another are some of the lessons taught to everyone in childhood. For example, most parts of the world have maps that show their region as being the center of the planet. The US is no different. No folks, the Americas are not at the center of the world, at least not according to maps in Europe, Japan, and many other places. Maps not only vary in organization, they vary in accuracy. Most maps used in education are drawn using a Mercatur projection which was developed to aid navigation several hundred years ago. This projection takes a spherical shape and flattens it, introducing tremendous distortion: zero distortion at the equator and absolute distortion at the poles. Although Greenland looks like a giant land mass on this map, in fact, it is only a third larger than Mexico. Most people's perception of these two countries' relative sizes is dead wrong. More accurate maps such as Buckminster Fuller's Dymaxion map have never caught on.

Food seems to be an area where biases and misinformation can bubble over as well. French toast does not exist by that name outside North America. Pastry popularly called "Danish" in the United Sates is called "Viennese" in Denmark. The "American" cookie, which is available in Germany and other countries, is almost impossible to find in the US.

Maps and food are internationally understood commodities but they vary greatly and can easily be mislabeled and and misunderstood. In this same way, a more modern international commodity like software can also be full of misinformation and bias.

Designers can often be ignorant about their own biases. Therefore, they are unable to filter out designs that will impact other people's national and cultural identity. They are also sometimes unwilling to investigate the international implications of their decisions. This can sometimes produce humorous results.

Photographs copyright© 1995 by Tony Fernandes

Figure ii-3 Pocari Sweat

For example, figure ii-3 shows a can of sweat. The product creators were trying to be cool but to most English speaking people, this Japanese product wouldn't be particularly appealing. The original name given to the Mitsubishi Montero, a 4 wheel drive vehicle, was the Pajero. It seemed to have a nice ring to it until Mitsubishi found out that pajero is Spanish for "masturbator." The Latin American market didn't approve. Coco, a perfume by Chanel, is the word for "crap" in Portuguese. When Coca Cola first went to China and wrote their name phonetically using kanji, the characters spelled out "bite the wax tadpole." There is a brand of toilet paper in Sweden named Kräpp. In Peru, Avon introduced a perfume called "crap" because it came packaged in a die. They came up with this name because it was the singular of "craps." They figured since craps is associated with two dice, crap would be appropriate for one. The list goes on and on. It's funny stuff but that wasn't the intention. The reason this happens is the designers and advertisers were blindsided by their own biases even with all the resources available to them as employees of the largest corporations in the world. Although these misunderstandings are funny, they also have a dark side.

In Hollywood movies, we often see stereotypes of people from different countries and laugh when there are misunderstandings because of cultural differences or language problems. But there's a very serious side to these misunderstandings as well. A young Japanese man was shot and killed in Louisiana because the homeowner of the door he was knocking on yelled "freeze!" and he only understood the word to mean "very cold". A man in Los Angeles was murdered because his shoe was pointing at a singer during a performance and it was considered very insulting. Recently, the clothing designer, Chanel, was threatened because one of the dresses she designed contained a glyph that resembled quotes from the Koran. And during the GATT negotiations that took place in 1993, France made the importation of American entertainment a big issue because they felt that their culture was being eroded by American movies. Although differences may seem laughable, it is important for product/ interface designers to realize that they can also be gravely serious. If some language and cultural misunderstanding can cause death, then designers of software products have a large responsibility indeed. A responsibility to learn about people, respect their way of life, and design products that will make them productive and not offend them.

Some people shrug these differences off. They point to the hope of homogenization the world through travel and communication. Often, the homogenizing comes in an American flavor; a flavor not everyone likes. Nationalism is on the increase especially in Europe. Maybe it is being driven by recession, or maybe it is being driven by the very effort to unite countries economically. According to my informal poll of European taxi drivers and bar tenders, from whom you can get some great truths, the increase of nationalism in Europe corresponds to the rise of the European Community. In other words, people are afraid of losing their cultural and national identity and are therefore reaffirming their belief systems and traditions. This type of sentiment has sometimes led to violence: It's powerful stuff.

Usability has become a hot button in the software market. Many companies pay a great deal of attention to how the product functions, how relevant the features are, and to the quality and legibility of the icons used. However, as people vary, so does the usability of the product. People approach problems differently, have needs unique to their location, and use everyday objects that differ from other parts of the world. Unfortunately, many software firms believe that one design with translated language is acceptable (usable) everywhere. Many companies are structured around this belief. Perhaps this is why many design methodologies have remained static although most software companies are selling internationally. Metaphors that rely on knowledge of the real world may not work because the real world varies, yet they are not being questioned. Icons that represent everyday objects in one country may present the user with obstacles because the objects may not exist in every part of the world. Yet, very few companies redesign their icons when software products get shipped overseas. Given all this, usability suffers for about 50% of most

American software companies' customers. Unhappy customers go elsewhere. This is why this issue is becoming increasingly important and the source of great competition.

Designers of the 90s need to understand that steps must be taken to acknowledge and deal with the numerous issues involved in designing for a country or culture that is not their own. The most important step of all is to realize that there is an issue: and it is a big issue. It is a issue that can only be understood and dealt with if you break down your misconceptions of the world as you know it and open yourself up to thinking of the interface design and development process in a whole new way. This book will present a collection of thoughts that will start you on your way.

It's time for a change.

Terminology

Terminology seems to be one of those issues that has ego associated with it. It seems like every presentation given regarding localization introduces new terminology or new semantics for old terminology. To simplify matters, let us begin with a discussion of the terms used in relation to this topic. The terms most used when discussing localization are:

- Globalization

- Internationalization (also sometimes known as I18N)

- Localization (also sometimes known as L12N)

- Nationalization

- Locale

These terms are often used interchangeably or are given meaning depending in the company's/speaker's point of view. Rather than trying to explain each of the factions out there and why they use certain terms, the following is a description of the terms used in this book.

Globalization - This is the process of creating a base design that can be changed or augmented for various countries/markets all over the world. It generally provides a set of "least common denominator" functionality. If a company develops a product with the same features for worldwide consumption, this can be viewed as a globalized product as well. A category of products that would succeed in taking this approach are utilities for certain pieces of hardware. In general, however, a "globalized" product refers to a set of easily localized functionality that can be modified and built upon to create designs and features unique to a country or culture.

1

Internationalization - Same as Globalization. This term will not be used.

I18N, L12N - These terms are monuments to the belief that this issue is just a technical one. I'd like to see these ridiculous terms go away. They needlessly mystify a fundamentally human problem with geeky use of numbers and text. They will not be used in this humble book.

Localization - A broad term that often takes into account all aspects of the international problem; both design and technical. This term refers to the process of making changes to a globalized product to make it usable and viable in a particular market. This is a great term but it often gets overused and made confusing. Because the discussion revolves around the context of design, this book will qualify the word "localization" to make it more specific. The term will be used in the following ways:

> **Technical localization** - This refers to the technical aspects of adapting a product to a foreign market such as double-byte conversion, operating system support, etc.
>
> **National localization** - This is a set of product behaviors/designs etc. that make it appropriate for a national setting. These designs enable the product to fully support all written language, punctuation, and formats and to solve the problems indigenous to a given nation. It is important to note that national localization is not merely translating the user interface to another language.
>
> **Cultural localization** - Beyond the notion of providing the correct functionality and the correct language, the issues of appeal, correctness, quality, and taste need to be dealt with as well. This is true not only to insure that the product is viewed as "attractive" but also that it doesn't communicate undesired messages. Cultural localization is the process of producing designs that are appropriate for a target culture's values, tastes, and history.

Now, onto the more interesting parts of this book.

Globalization: Laying the Groundwork

The way the home computer came together has caused many fundamental problems for user interfaces and their viability internationally. The present GUIs (Graphical User Interfaces) are so full of metaphors, symbols, and assumptions about formats, and language that it makes it impossible to design one interface/product that will work throughout the world unless it does so by providing many languages simultaneously.

An exception to this problem is applications that use a universally understood set of symbols: for example, electrical symbols, architectural elements, etc., as well as products that deal with a specific computer related issues such as memory management. These types of products are much more easily standardized than most other applications.

The problem comes down to four areas that are particularly problematic for user interfaces:

1. Language
2. Visual communication
3. Appropriateness of features
4. Taste

Because these variations are so great, it is important to lay a foundation that can handle change very easily. Then, the foundation needs to be built upon with a great deal of knowledge of the target users. Globalization represents the creation of code and a UI (User Interface) design foundation that will work internationally or on which local designs can be implemented. The globalization process has two inseparable components: UI design and code issues. Both must be dealt with in order to make this very important base viable. No matter what form the product ultimately takes, and to which countries it is shipped, globalization must begin from day one. If it isn't built in, it will put a team of people in the same situation as Ginger Rogers: that is, doing everything that Fred Astaire did but backwards and in high heels.

Attributes of a successful globalization process

It is the desire of most major software companies to make a single product work worldwide. This desire is an economic one. It is cheaper to just have one product that gets sent everywhere. Of course, that isn't always realistic. To solve this problem, you can take one of two extreme approaches. One is to cram every little difference into a single product. Of course taking this approach makes the product complex to use because users must constantly deal with features that are totally useless to them. At the other extreme, you only ship with the features and designs that work for everyone. Not only can this set of features be small, it can also produce a solution that pleases nobody. The answer lies somewhere in the middle.

Inherent in the terms described in the previous chapter is a process. Ideally, the process begins with a great deal of knowledge about the target nation, the target customers, and the problems that the product will try to solve: classic user interface stuff. Unfortunately, the classic process for designing user interfaces goes something like this:

- Design and develop a domestic version as quickly as possible and get it out the door.

- The interface designer forgets about the product.

- Developers go back to make the product technically localizable thereby delaying shipment to foreign countries by several months or years.

- Throw the product "over the wall" to another organization in the company or an outside localization firm to do the actual translation and localization.

- Hope that what comes of the other side is remotely usable by people in other nations.

The problems with this process are:

- It's expensive. A great deal of code is written several times.

- No international expertise is injected into the primary creators of the product. This insures that this cycle will repeat itself release after release.

- The UI design may lose a large amount of its usability because most principles and guidelines are not communicated effectively to the new organization. The interface may also communicate poor quality due to changes that were introduced without the insight of the product's original designer(s).

- The product will suffer in foreign markets because of large delays.

Companies operating in this model will not be able to compete effectively with those that are producing world-ready designs from the start. The process should be

- Identify all target cultures.

- Design and develop a global base that takes common designs into account.

- An interface designer to oversees the design of all localized versions of the product.

- Conduct usability tests of localized versions.

Transition to the latter approach will cause many changes in the way projects are run and organized. For interface designers, the most profound change is that now he or she must design a product with the full knowledge of the target audiences, both domestic and international, and the designer must continue to influence the product after the shipment of the domestic version.

Corporate culture

A company must have commitment from the top to make the endeavor of designing for international markets a success. Management has to believe that localizing is important to its future and it needs to communicate that fact to the ranks. Thinking as an international company must permeate all parts of the company. Without this, the right code won't get written, the right schedules won't be developed, the right amount of marketing resources won't be committed, and the right product will not be produced.

In addition to the communication from up on high, there have to be visible vestiges of the international attitude. Claris Corporation offers an example of how this is done well. Claris published a booklet for its customers in which it spells out its values and where it sees itself going. One of the sections, along with technology and all the other things you would expect from a software company, spells out its belief in the global marketplace and how it is conducting its business to compete in it (figure 2-1). Claris lists "customers" and their support as one of its corporate values. The image of the customers that is seen all over the company's campus shows people around a globe. The environment continually reinforces the fact that it is producing international products.

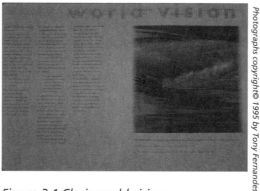

Photographs copyright© 1995 by Tony Fernandes

Figure 2-1 Claris world vision

Microsoft's Dublin facility has a localization philosophy that symbolizes the global attitude as well. It is represented in the acronym EIJAL (English is just another language). That is a great example of global thinking.

Before success can be achieved in the world of localization and global design, the culture in which it is done must not only support localization, it must nurture it.

Technical expertise

One of the big payoffs of this culture is in the code that is written. Without a great code base that can be easily changed and augmented, developing relevant designs becomes impossible. Unfortunately, there are many products still being written with localization as an afterthought. Engineers of the global or domestic versions of products must begin to gain expertise in building in localization. Like quality, localization must be built in from the start; it cannot be added as an afterthought. Many of the language issues boil down to technical considerations. To get a sense of what those issues are, refer to Appendix B.

Great communication

No matter how a company is organized, it must have good communication channels between all parities involved. If a localized version of a product is going to be produced by an organization other than the original product group, that outside organization should be involved from the very inception of the project. They should receive regular updates of the product as it is being developed and they should be given full access to the same resources and people that wrote the base version. Of course, it is important that the people they talk to know about the issues involved in localizing. This ties directly into the previous two issues, technical expertise and corporate values.

Design rule 1: Design a global base

A design should be developed that acts as a base for all other designs. All of this assumes a code base that is technically able to be easily adapted. Appendix B offers some insight into how to create a technical localization effort. Three interface design approaches can be taken in designing a global base.

1. All-inclusive: All features and variations of features are consolidated into one version that is shipped everywhere with different defaults. An example of this is a graphics product that ships with a ruler in centimeters and a ruler in inches. The default ruler in Europe would be centimeters and the default ruler in the US and Canada would be inches.

2. Model design: A design is developed that acts as a model for all products, certain parts of which are replaced or modified. For example, a product may ship with a calendar feature but the calendar code is modified to correspond to each of the target countries.

3. A combination of the previous two methods.

Regardless of which approach is taken, each requires the interface designer to have a reasonable understanding of the target countries and cultures.

Identify target locales
A list should be made of all the countries and regions the product is targeted at. Right from the start, it should be clear to all members of a project group that the product is international. This knowledge will aid people in making decisions about their work. Localization, after all, will impact not only the interface designer and the developers but also documentation, operations, and QA.

Gather information about the target locales
Once the list is made, information regarding these countries and their cultures should be distributed to all the members of the group.

Issues this large and this human defy the notion of rules and guidelines. Nevertheless, in order to create a framework for designers to work from, I will present the material in the form of design rules. These rules will provide the designer with a set of issues to ponder and discuss before and during their design phase. They also serve as a tool to evaluate existing products.

7

The chapters that follow provide a good deal of information about what differs between locales all around the world.

Determine the target audience

With the target locales set, the target audience in each locale must be determined. Be aware that the target market, and therefore user base, may vary from country to country. For example, a product that was created for novice draw users in one country may be more appropriate as a business product for computer-literate professionals in another. It must be clear who the target audience is for each target locale.

With this knowledge, you can begin to piece together a picture of what will and won't work internationally. Now comes the time to design a global base that capitalizes on this knowledge.

Know who you are designing for. It's the only way.

Dealing with language

Language and globalizing don't seem to mix on the surface. People speak many different languages all over the world so there is no "global" language solution. The next best thing is to take an all-inclusive approach to the design: Provide all the languages in one product. This philosophy can be found in many consumer products, as shown in figure 2-2.

Figure 2-2 Nikon documentation
Photographs copyright© 1995 by Tony Fernandes

The all-inclusive approach can be made to work if the target locales are determined and their languages identified. This creates the possibility of shipping a product that gives the user a choice of languages to run the product with, as shown in figure 2-3.

Figure 2-3 Adobe Type On Call
Courtesy of Adobe

If you take this approach, make sure you do it correctly. Note that the buttons in figure 2-3 are written in their respective languages: this is the correct way to do it. Writing all the buttons in English makes no sense but it nevertheless happens as shown in figure 2-4. In addition, there are techniques that will reduce the amount of text that appears.

Reduce the number of commands

Try to reduce some interface dependencies by reducing the amount of commands that must be issued.

The more gestures and direct manipulation your product has, the better. Some great examples of this philosophy are interfaces that use drag and drop functionality. In Microsoft Word, for example, a piece of text can be selected and moved to another point by using the mouse without the user issuing any menu commands or clicking on icons that may need to be localized.

In general, the more empowered the user is with his or her mouse, the easier the interface will be to localize. **!**

Use visual feedback

Feedback can also play an important part in simplifying the interfaces. By using the cursor and other visual elements to convey states, the amount of text that the user sees is reduced.

In reality, interfaces with any kind of complexity will not be able to ship with every language. In most cases, the model approach, in which the product is modified for every language, must be used. By reducing the amount of text and increasing the amount of direct manipulation, however, you will not only make translation easier, you will wind up with a better UI all around.

Figure 2-4 "Just Grandma and Me" Courtesy of Broderbund

Visual communication

The whole idea of using icons on the computer was to convey ideas, hopefully internationally, without text. Unfortunately, the icons have historically been defined with bits and pieces of the real world: a world that is redefined from country to country.

If history could be rolled back, it would have made much more sense to develop a unique visual language that allowed people to use the computer as an information appliance. This language would employ a set of culturally neutral symbols and gestures that would allow all people of the world to learn one common set of commands and icons. Tape recorders went through a similar process of developing the set of controls that are now found on VCRs and even in some software products as shown in figure 2-5.

Figure 2-5 Controls from Macromedia Director
Courtesy Macromedia

Icons are used to communicate ideas. While some symbols work internationally, others don't. By maximizing the use of images that work in all your target locales, it will take less time to localize the interface and the product will be similar to other localized versions all over the world.

International visual design can be done well. Some of the best examples can be found at international sporting events such as the World Cup. The signs that direct you to the stadiums, figure 2-6, couldn't have been simpler. They got you there regardless of your language.

Figure 2-6 Directions to stadium

Likewise, the signs for getting a bus and getting information were equally clear, as shown in figures 2-7 and 2-8.

Figure 2 7   Bus stop

Figure 2-8 Information

Make use of international images

For your interface, make sure you use everyday objects that work internationally as well as international symbols. Some of the objects that are recognizable around the world include:

Be aware that although these objects are recognizable, they may signify different things. For example, a lightbub is internationally recognizable as a light source but it is not always associated with having an idea.

Light bulbs
Telephones
Books
Envelopes
Computers
Flashlight
Nature
Tools
Umbrellas
The globe
Binoculars
Eyeglasses
Scissors
Audio speakers
VCR/tape controls
Microphones
Arrows
Magnifying glasses
Trains, cars, boats, and transportation
A smile and a frown

Certain domains such as architecture and electronics use the same symbols internationally. If the product is intended for a specialized field, make use of any and all international norms in that area.

Remove text from icons

Removing as much text as possible from the user interface may increase the amount of the design that will work internationally. Icons in particular are bad news when they contain text. First, they will have to be edited with a bitmap editor for each locale. Second, words from large languages will not be able to fit into the space provided. As you can see in figure 2-9(a), icons from CE Software's QuickMail have text that is a very tight fit in English, One way of getting around this problem is to use a form of balloon help: first popularized by the Mac. This method will present the user with text explaining the icon without imbedding it. Figure 2-9(b) shows a feature of this type in action in Lotus Approach. The message only appears when the user's mouse stops over the icon. In this way, text is provided but independent of size contraints in the body of the icon.

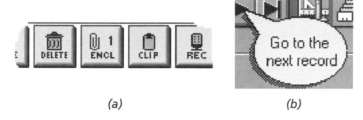

(a)   (b)

Figure 2-9 Text descriptions for icons
Coutesy of QE Software and Lotus Development Corp.

Knowledge about the differences between target users allows you to create local designs. The local designs take into account the process of developing a national design as well as a cultural design. During this creation process, new features and interaction styles are designed.

Feature appropriateness

As in any interface design, field research should be done to learn about the target audience's terminology and needs. With this knowledge, features should be evaluated for appropriateness.

Assess which features will stay identical
Some features will operate identically but using other languages. For example, users in all countries will have to open files, print, as well as many other common actions that are appropriate to the particular problem domain. These portions of the UI will need less attention than others.

Determine which designs will need to be tweaked
Domain-specific features may be viable for all countries but their specific design and implementation may vary. For example, a feature that helps address envelopes may be needed for all target countries but the number of fields, their positions, and the navigation from field to field may have to be redesigned.

Determine what needs to be thrown out and what needs to be created
Given the processes present in the target nations, make a determination about what features may have to be completely rethought or

removed. For example, a spreadsheet feature that automates the writing of a US 1040 tax form is a good candidate for removal when the product is shipped to other countries.

Developing a global base is a necessary exercise to lay the groundwork for the local versions. The net effect is a least common denominator, however. The chapters that follow dive into the world of creating a viable solution for locales around the world.

National Language

Language is a beautiful and wondrous thing that has developed over countless generations in various parts of the world. Language is fundamental to human communication and has been for all of recorded history. That explains why so many people are attached to their own. There are great differences between languages that developed completely independently of each other such as Japanese and Swedish, for example. There are lesser differences between languages that developed from a common base, such as Latin, but there are differences nevertheless. If this were an encyclopedia sized book, we could get into the specifics of each one. Because that's not the case, this chapter will examine the ways in which languages differ and how those differences impact user interfaces.

The national localization of a user interface involves many aspects and fulfills several missions. No matter what country the user interface is designed for, however, it must do the following:

- Communicate in the country's native language

- Support the natural writing symbols, punctuation, etc.

- Support native date, currency, weight scales, numbers, and addresses

- Support natural work habits and the work environment

- Communicate in an inoffensive manner

The latter two points are partially cultural issues. They will be covered more thoroughly in the "Cultural Localization" chapter.

In looking at this list, it might appear that the first two items are the most straightforward. In fact, they pose some of the greatest challenges.

Language is important because it involves a basic need: communication. Since the process of using a software product is inherently a process of communication, language, especially written language, must be handled well. It is also the first step in national localization.

Design Rule 2: Provide the correct language

It sounds easy enough. There are enormous obstacles to overcome, however. What is needed above all else in dealing with this issue is knowledge of the variations found in the earth's languages.

Scripts

Languages are written using one of several scripts. These scripts are a collection of characters and glyphs that represent a written rendition of a spoken language. The most popular scripts are (roughly ordered by amount of speakers):

- Roman - English and other European languages
- Kanji - China, Japan, and other countries of Asia
- Cyrillic - Russia and Eastern Europe
- Arabic - Middle East
- Kana - Japan
- Devanagari - India
- Korean - Korea
- Bengali - India
- Thai - Thailand
- Telugu -India

Many examples given below involve Japanese. This is because Japanese scripts offer a stark contrast to languages that use the Roman alphabet exclusively. Japan is also a large market for US-made software.

Other notable scripts include Burmese, Greek, and Hebrew.

Using the correct written language is a powerful tool in maintaining the usability of a product. As is shown in figures 3-1 and 3-2, the resulting differences have a tremendous visual impact on the user interface and immediately turn it into something associated with a particular region of the world.

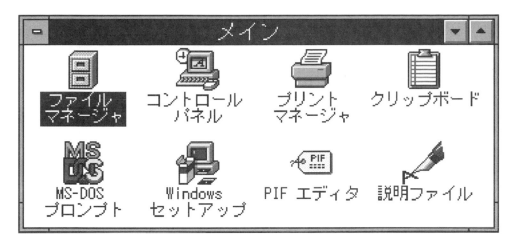

Figure 3-1 Microsoft Windows J
Courtesy of Microsoft

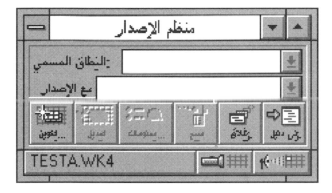

Figure 3-2 Lotus 1-2-3 for Windows, Arabic
Courtesy of Lotus Development Corp.

One of the exceptions to the rule of proving the correct written language is when it comes to trademarked names. Those must appear in the original language in many instances.

Size

Scripts can be divided into two main categories: large and small systems[1]. Large scripts have thousands of written symbols. An example of a large system would be Chinese with its approximately 10,000 symbols (some estimates go to 22,000 symbols). Other large systems include Japanese and Korean. A small system has less than 200 characters and is typically based on the Roman alphabet. The English alphabet is considered a small system with its 26-character alphabet.

The number of characters becomes a technical as well as a UI design issue. The UI will have to support the input of characters that are specified by multiple keypresses. This is because most reasonably sized keyboards can't support the convention of a single key per symbol.

Multiple writing systems

In some situations, there is only one spoken language but there are multiple writing systems to represent it. Japan is a country where this is true. There you will regularly find the Roman alphabet, hiragana, katakana, and kanji used. Kanji, shown in figure 3-3(c) originated in China and is used in several Pacific Rim countries including China, Japan, and Korea. They fall into the category of pictographs: each glyph is a picture that represents an idea. Although the same symbols are used, the pronunciations vary. Hiragana, figure 3-3(b), uses glyphs that represent syllables. Katakana, figure 3-3(a), also represents syllables and it is typically used to write words borrowed from other languages. As shown in figure 3-4, in many cases, they are all intermixed.

Katakana and hiragana are collectively known as kana.

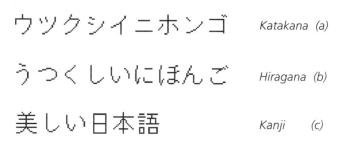

ウツクシイニホンゴ   *Katakana (a)*

うつくしいにほんご   *Hiragana (b)*

美しい日本語   *Kanji (c)*

Figure 3-3 Japanese scripts

Any word processor for the Japanese market would need to support all four scripts.

Make sure you understand the number of scripts that need to be supported in your target locale.

Multiple languages

Providing the correct written language for a target country may mean providing support for several languages. For example, the languages used in Belgium are French and Dutch. The Swiss use German, French, Italian, and others. Canadians use English and French.

Photographs copyright© 1995 by Tony Fernandes

Figure 3-4 Sign in Japan

On a larger scale, business in Europe can often require users to work in many languages although they may only need one in their native countries.

One interesting approach to this problem can be found in the Accent word processor from Accent Software International of Israel. This product presents the user with the ability to change languages by simply selecting one from a popup as shown in figure 3-5. The fonts are automatically adjusted and so is the dictionary. In addition, the user may select what language they would like the user interface to be presented in. The choices include languages using Roman scripts as well as others. Figure 3-6 shows the user interface presented in Russian in the Cyrillic script. Notice that the interface is independent of the language being written. In figure 3-6, the language popup indicates that French is being written.

In order to truly cater to the needs of the international customer, the interface includes translation tools to help users get from one language to another as well as spell checking for various languages, as shown in figure 3-7.

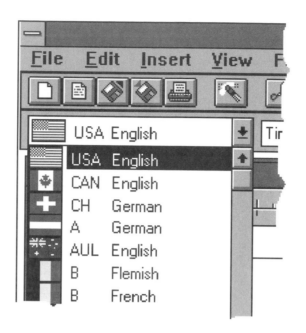

Figure 3-5 A choice of languages
Courtesy of Accent Software

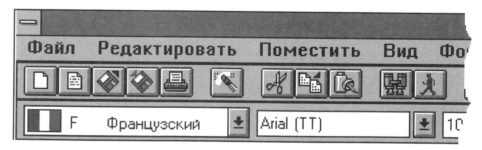

Figure 3-6 The interface running in Russian
Courtesy of Accent Software

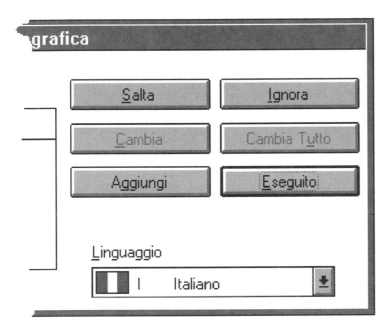

Figure 3-7 Spell checking Italian
Courtesy of Accent Software

If the interface cannot handle the language issue as thoroughly as Accent, at least it can facilitate the typing of foreign characters. Microsoft Word does this by providing an icon in its toolbar shown in figure 3-8 which allows the user to have access to all the characters available in the operating system version they are running. When the icon is pressed, a table appears giving the user access to characters of the native script which quite often include significant variations of certain letters such as A and E. In figure 3-9, the set of characters for the Roman alphabet running in the English language version of the Mac operating system are shown.

Figure 3-8 Microsoft Word's
access to characters
Courtesy of Microsoft

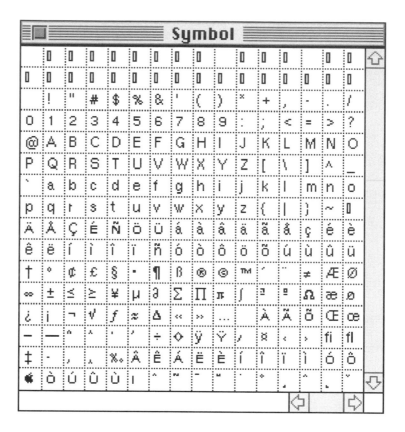

Figure 3-9 Character selection in Microsoft Word
Courtesy of Microsoft

If the user interface produces ready-made material and it is intended to ship in a locale that has several languages, user's should be allowed to select the language they want the output to appear in. As shown in figure 3-10, Microsoft Publisher is well suited for the European market because all its content, such as calenders, can be produced in a language of the user's choice.

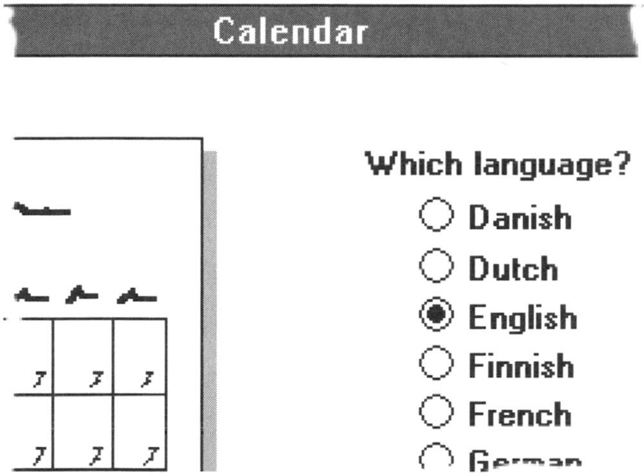

Calendar

Which language?
- ○ Danish
- ○ Dutch
- ◉ English
- ○ Finnish
- ○ French
- ○ German

Figure 3-10 Microsoft Publisher
Courtesy of Microsoft

In some cases, support for multiple languages is provided at the operating system level. WorldScript from Apple Computer is a technology that allows the Mac OS to support multiple languages simultaneously. This is done through "Language Kits" and by running WorldScript enabled applications. This is very handy when you have to put different scripts on the same printed page as is found in this book. Products such as NisusWriter from Nisus Software, figure 3-11, do an excellent job of providing access to multiple scripts simultaneously by using this technology. The number of scripts it provides to the user is limited only by the availability of operating system language kits. This is a great way to deal with documents that may need to mix an unforeseen number of languages on the same page.

The advantage of having this work at the OS level is that no special interface issues are introduced. It also allows users to use their favorite applications to complete their work. Nisus also sells language kits for its product that include spelling and hyphenation dictionaries, thesaurus, and keyboard layout files.

Dialect

As if all the differences mentioned above were not enough to worry about, there is still the matter of dialect. It's important to realize that many languages are not standardized: From one common source, they have evolved differently in different locales. As George Bernard Shaw said, "England and America are two countries divided by a

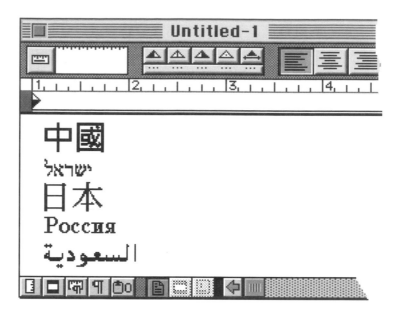

Figure 3-11. NisusWriter from Nisus Software
Courtesy of Nisus Software

common language." As it is true between the US and Britain, so it is for other parts of the world. So for example, the trash can on the Macintosh desktop is called the rubbish can in Australia and the wastebasket in England. These changes in dialect, etc., are extremely relevant to user interface design. For example, when I was on business in Portugal, I discovered that the English version of a famous word processor was outselling the localized Portuguese version. The reason was that the product was localized into Brazilian Portuguese rather than Continental Portuguese. This was problematic for the market. To get a clue as to why that is, you have to go back to the history of the Portuguese Empire and realize that Brazil was Portugal's penal colony. So, here you have a product written in a language that is the same yet has words and expressions that are considered unbusinesslike. To get an idea of this effect in English, imagine using a product with Caribbean pirate phrases such as "Hoist up the file." A similar effect can happen between European Spanish and Western Spanish, as well as French and Canadian French.

Bazilians have no love for continental Portuguese in return.

 When planning a product for a target country, you need to provide not only the correct language, you also need to provide it in the correct dialect.

If the locale uses several languages, make sure they are all supported in the user interface.

!

Design rule 3: Physical variations should be taken into account

Once the target languages and scripts have been determined for your target locales, the interfaces must be able to deal with the physical impact of all the variations they represent. Below are some of the variations that will impact the user interface the most.

Direction

Written language can be bidirectional or unidirectional. English is an example of a unidirectional script: It is written from left to right. Scripts such as kana are also unidirectional but the direction can be top to bottom, as shown in figure 3-12, or left to right, as shown in figure 3-13. A bidirectional script, such as Arabic, can be written from right to left, and in certain situations such as numbers, written from left to right.

Figure 3-12 shows an example from Japan where you can see how text is written vertically in an ad, and figure 3-13 shows text written horizontally on the cover of a book.

Figure 3-12 An ad for Riviera Bank

Figure 3-14 gives you a visual representation of the differences. The arrowhead at the end of the line indicates the starting point. The lines indicate the track of the eyes as they read. The arrowheads in the body indicate the reading direction.

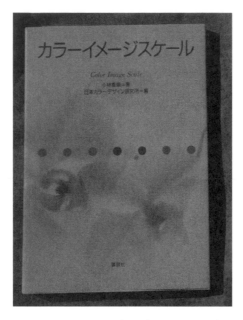

Figure 3-13 Cover of "Color Image Scale"

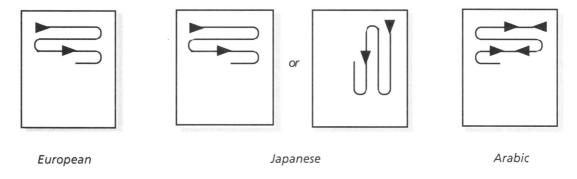

European   Japanese   Arabic

Figure 3-14 Reading directions for various languages

In Adobe Illustrator for Japan, support for writing vertically is included in the product. The functionality is accessible through the right-most icon in figure 3-15.

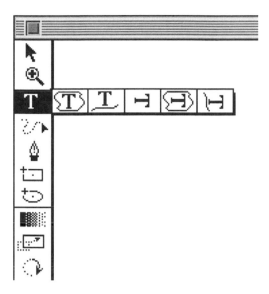

Figure 3-15 Adobe Illustrator
Courtesy of Adobe

The icon indicates that text would appear as shown in figure 3-16(a) when, in reality, it would write the text as shown in figure 3-16(b). This is a classic usability problem brought about by a bias regarding how Roman letters would typically be presented.

(a)   (b)

Figure 3-16 Text orientation

Right-to-left languages are a tremendous challenge because they require that all left-to-right conventions be replaced in the interface. Lotus 1-2-3 for Windows-Arabic gives a good example of how to deal with this problem. Figure 3-17 shows how the English language version of the Lotus 1-2-3 for Windows spreadsheet looks.

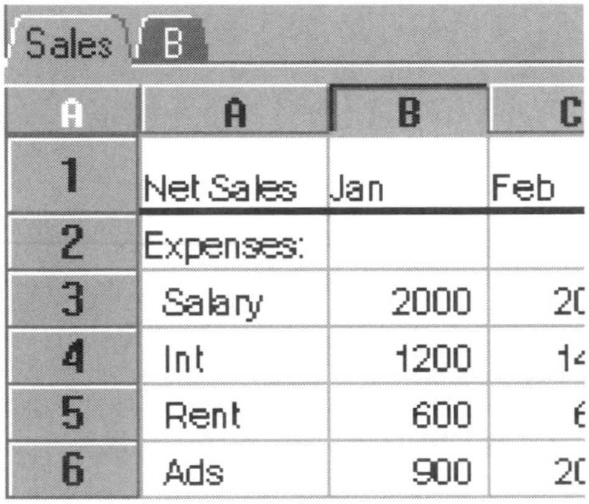

Sales	B		
A	**A**	**B**	**C**
1	Net Sales	Jan	Feb
2	Expenses:		
3	Salary	2000	2(
4	Int	1200	1₄
5	Rent	600	€
6	Ads	900	2(

Figure 3-17 Lotus 1-2-3 for Windows Courtesy of Lotus Development Corp.

In order to present the same interface to a user that reads right to left, the whole interface has to be turned around. That is precisely what Lotus did, as shown in figure 3-18. Not only is the text in the cells flowing from right to left, the spreadsheet tabs are on the right, the columns increment from right to left, and the row numbers are presented along the right.

Note that the numbers are written in Arabic. What people in the west call Arabic numerals are not used in Arabic locales.

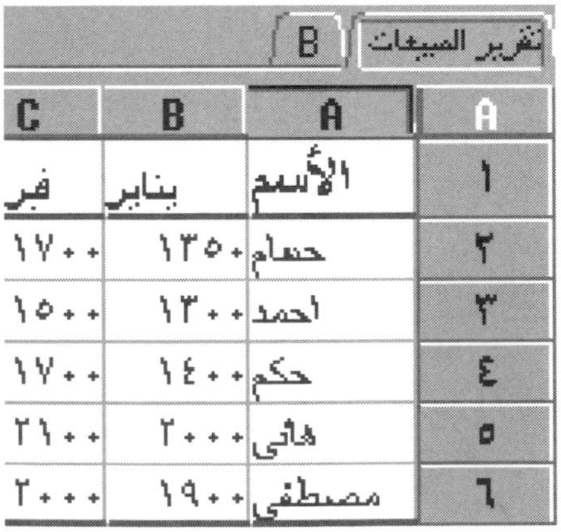

	B	تقرير المبيعات	
C	**B**	**A**	**A**
فبر	يناير	الأسم	١
١٧٠٠	١٢٥٠	حسام	٢
١٥٠٠	١٢٠٠	احمد	٣
١٧٠٠	١٤٠٠	حكم	٤
٢١٠٠	٢٠٠٠	هانى	٥
٢٠٠٠	١٩٠٠	مصطفى	٦

Figure 3-18 Lotus 1-2-3 for Window Arabic Courtesy of Lotus Development Corp.

The interface wouldn't be translated correctly if it didn't deal with the menus as well. As you can see in figure 3-19, even the menus are reversed relative to the English version.

Figure 3-19 Arabic and English versions of the menu Courtesy of Lotus Development Corp.

Make sure the interface deals with all aspects of language direction.

!

Insertion points

The insertion point, where the next character will appear once a key is pressed, moves along in front of the first character you type. With a bidirectional language, however, the insertion point will move right or left depending on what you are typing. Depending on the application you are designing, some special considerations may have to be given to control the insertion point.

Hyphenation

Hyphenation was an idea borne out of necessity in the European typesetting industry. It was important to keep the right margin looking neat so something had to be done with those huge words. The solution was to allow words to be split at the syllabic boundaries. For example, "difference" could be split at three points: dif-fer-ence. The only problem is that this type of rule does not work for all Roman script languages. In German, for example, hyphenation can actually change the spelling of words. For example, "ck" becomes "kk" when split: Zucker turns to Zuk-ker.

Japanese can have breaks anywhere with the exception of where some punctuation appears. If there are words breaks, a hyphen is not used. In Arabic, word splitting is disallowed so no hyphenation is necessary.

Don't assume that the same hyphenation rules apply to all languages.

!

Stressing

The way words are stressed varies. Languages written in Roman script use underlining, boldface, italicizing, and capitalizing to stress a word. When dealing with the Japanese scripts, stressing is provided in several ways. One method is to use amikake, as shown in figure 3-20. This stressing method calls attention to a section of text by putting a background rectangle behind it.

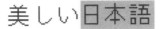

Figure 3-20 Amikake

Where bullets might be used along the left side of English text, in Japan, they would be used in a slightly different place, as shown in figure 3-21. This techniquc is called wakiten.

Figure 3-21 Wakiten

These styles need to be supported in Japanese word processing products if they are to be competitive. Figures 3-23 and 3-24 show popup menus in ClarisImpact J that support both of the previous examples. Note that, in the amikake example, users are given the opportunity to specify what shade they would like their amikake in.

Fonts

As scripts vary, so do the standard fonts that can render them. Being conscious of fonts is important because they influence layout issues in the interface, in sample files, and in content in general. Assumptions that fonts of the same point size will be rendered in approximately the same size is wrong. This is particularly true when dealing with symbols from the Pacific Rim and Japan.

Certain scripts have constructs that go beyond simply placing one symbol after another in a row or column. An example of this is Japanese furigana, as shown in figure 3-22. There are small characters above or below other symbols that aid the reader in pronouncing the associated symbol . This type of annotation is often used in children's books or when a relatively unknown kanji symbol is used.

More will be discussed about fonts in the "Cultural Aesthetics" chapter.

うつく　　に ほん ご
美 し い 日 本 語

Figure 3-22 Furigana (ruby text)

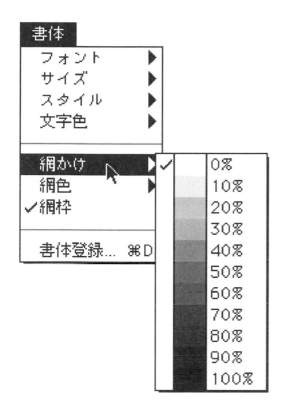

Figure 3-23 Amikake support in ClarisImpact J
Courtesy of Claris

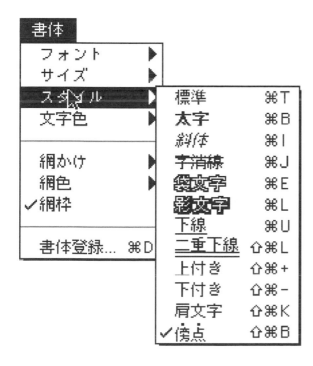

Figure 3-24 Wakiten support In ClarisImpact J
Courtesy of Claris

Products such as Ventura Publisher J provide the user with the ability to create furigana. Not every product does because it is a technical and design nightmare

Layouts

English, European, and some forms of Japanese are well suited to the usual dialog box layout conventions. They are laid out with text flowing left to right with the pushbuttons somewhere on the right bottom or top. For languages that flow from right to left, the layout will have to be completely reversed. If you find yourself looking at button placement guidelines that suggest that pushbuttons be in a certain place no matter what, recognize that some of these rules were written with only English in mind. In figure 3-25, the Mac Find dialog box is shown. Figure 3-26 shows the same dialog box but laid out correctly to accommodate the reading direction of Arabic.

It is often the case that the final layout of a localized product is done by someone other than the original interface designer. If this is the case, make sure that whoever is doing the work uses the same set of guidelines. Often, localizing professionals are not skilled in visual design and produce extremely ugly layouts that affect the product's usability.

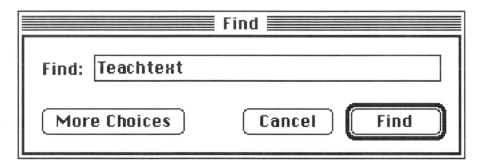

Figure 3-25 English Mac Find Courtesy of Apple Computer

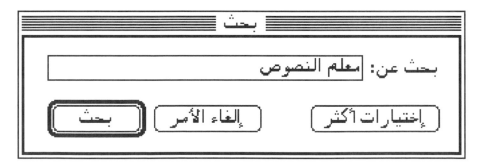

Figure 3-26 Arabic Mac Find Courtesy of Apple Computer

The size of words also influences the layout of dialog boxes. German words are generally much longer and will need more space. If your layouts are tight, they will have to be reworked to handle longer words. Typically, German words can be 30% longer than the equivalent English word.

There are two possible approaches for dealing with this:

1. Readjust all dialog box layouts after the translation. This can be done either by the original interface designers or by an outside party with a well-written set of layout guidelines.

2. Allow room for expansion. By allowing your dialog boxes and status areas to have extra room, little adjustment will have to be made after translation.

Adjust the layout of the interface to accommodate different directions and size changes. **!**

Dialog box sentence structure

Interface designers are always looking to make dialog boxes as easy as possible to understand. A technique that allows you to make the flow through a dialog box obvious is to structure it in the form of a sentence, as shown in figure 3-27.

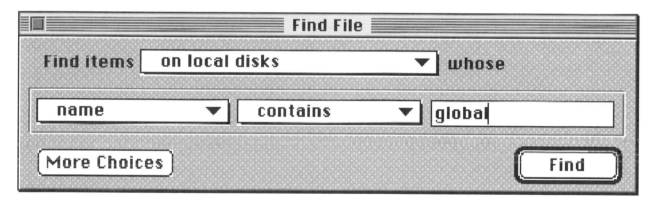

Figure 3-27 Dialog box with a sentence structure

The only problem is that this layout and number of controls make the following assumptions:

*   The sentence has adjectives, verbs, and nouns in the same places for all languages.

*   The sentence can only be expressed using a fixed number of words.

• What is being searched for appears last in the sentence.

 If you are going to use sentence structures, you must be willing to rework the dialog box to match sentence constructs of other languages.

Metaphors

Since the direction of the text varies, so does the orientation of a book. Western books have the spine on the left and the pages are turned right to left. Arabic books have the spine on the right and have the pages turned left to right. This is also true for Japanese and Chinese books/magazines written with vertical text, as shown in figure 3-28.

As a side note, by Western convention, all chapters begin on the page to the right.

Figure 3-28 Spine on the right Courtesy of Mono Magazine

If your interface is based on a book metaphor, realize that the flow of pages will have to be reversed for certain countries and applications.

Text justification

The notion of text justification varies. In Roman script languages, text is usually left, center, or right justified. In Japan, justification has some other twists. For example, text can justified "wide" or "narrow." Figure 3-29 shows a menu item from ClarisImpact J that lets the user space the text out to fill space. This is common in diagrams such as organization charts. The second line in figure 3-30 is "wide" justified.

There are various Japanese justification methods. In general, text is fully justified. Kissoku justification, however, forces changes that cause other techniques to come into play. In case you will deal with this issue, find out about shukoshou and burasage.

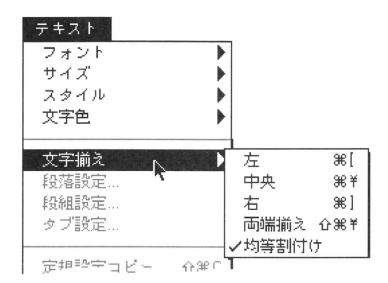

Figure 3-29 Text justification in ClarisImpact J Courtesy of Claris

Figure 3-30 Position in an organization chart Courtesy of Claris

Other layout issues
Tables written in languages that are read from right to left will have the labels along the right and the values trailing off to the left. Keep this in mind with any feature that assumes labels along the left side. An example of this would be styles.

Text sort orders
Even in languages that use the same script, sort orders vary. For example in Spanish, cho comes after co because ch is treated as a single character. In Finnish, A is the first letter but Å comes after Z. In French, Å comes after A.

In Japanese, there are various sort orders such as the "poem" order. This is an ordering based on an ancient poem. Also, sorting of people in a company is done alphabetically but within levels of management.

One approach is to change the sort order for the alphabet used in the target locale. Some products take the all-inclusive approach and allow words and information from a variety of countries to be handled in one file. In FileMaker Pro, a data base product from Claris, the sort dialog box has a popup, figure 3-31, that allows the users to select what sorting rules they would like to use on the information, figure 3-32. This allows the user to sort the information for a variety of languages. It allows the interface to stay the same for each country, with the only change being the default sort order.

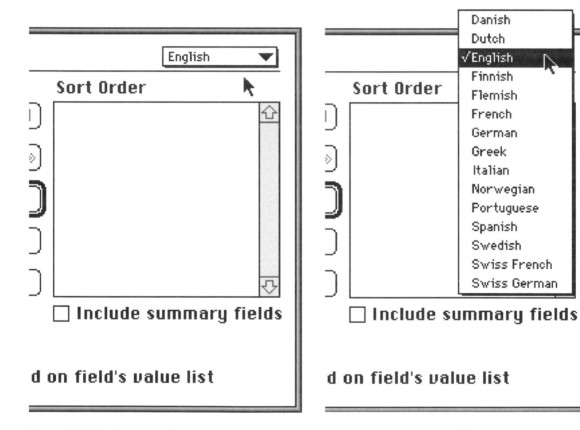

Figure 3-31 Sorting control

Figure 3-32 Sorting control open both *Courtesy of Claris*

Visual Language

Spanish is certainly another major language spoken in the US.

In addition to written text, computers also communicate by visual means. Visual communication is an issue bigger than international design. The discussion in this chapter will concentrate on the situation created when visual designs inadvertently carry biases borne out of the designer's knowledge of their own language.

Most Americans don't deal with a large amount of visual communication. Perhaps this is because, unlike other parts of the world, there are very few other languages that compete with English. This has made English text an acceptable vehicle for communication in most instances.

An obvious example of this philosophy is American traffic signs. They are very textual. Although this is beginning to change, American signage has a poor tradition in visual communication. Signs quite often assume that not only do viewers read English, they are also knowledgeable of American abbreviations. This attitude persists even in situations where it is known that foreign visitors are present and danger is near. For example, the sign in figure 4-1 is in front of the White House in Washington, DC. The reason it is there is because you never know when a limousine will come racing around the corner as part of a motorcade. When it says "DON'T WALK," the limousine drivers assume that the crosswalks are clear. Therefore, it is required that pedestrians press the button and wait for the "WALK" sign. The sign is only written in English. The walk sign that the button press would turn on is also in English. Language bias can be a dangerous thing.

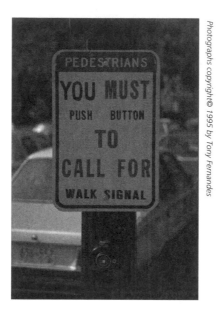

Photographs copyright© 1995 by Tony Fernandes

Figure 4-1 Sign at White House

Significant signs that only use English text can be found on practically every street of the US. Figure 4-2 shows one that is all too familiar. Put yourself in the shoes of a visitor trying to get about in the US. Unless you know English, it is very easy to break the law in the United States.

Of course, some signs do use images. They often come with ridiculous abbreviations, however. Figure 4-3 shows the US pedestrian crossing sign that uses the abbreviation "PED XINGS." X is often used to abbreviate "cross" but that is only understood in the US and Canada. Ped is Latin for foot so this sign could have some creative interpretations.

Even in situations where an idea could have been easily communicated with a picture, American signs opt for text. In figure 4-4, it isn't clear whether this sign is warning the driver of a hazard or whether it is calling them a name.

In other regions of the world, visual communication is much more mature and accepted. Contrast the design philosophy between the typical American "WALK" sign in figure 4-5 and the European equivalent in figure 4-6: The embodiment of a textual vs. visual approach to communication.

Figure 4-2 An unpopular sign

Figure 4-3 US pedestrian sign

Figure 4-4 The big DIP

Figure 4-5 American walk sign

Figure 4-6 European walk sign   *Figure 4-7 European "No Parking" sign*

Contrast the European "No Parking" sign shown in figure 4-7 with the American equivalent in figure 4-2. A clear cause and effect is illustrated in the European version which leaves no doubt what will happen if you park at this particular spot. Note the design of the "no parking" sign itself: a circular form that is easily spotted even in bad weather.

While circular signs indicate laws in Europe, the triangular signs indicate warnings. Again, in the warning sign shown in figure 4-8, it is clear what the danger is. It is also clear what will happen to you if you ignore the warning.

Even exit signs have a graphical design showing a person and door as shown in figure 4-9. Rather than the classic textual American "EXIT" sign written in red, the European sign is designed using green to indicate safe passage.

Figure 4-8 Warning in Amsterdam

Figure 4-9 Exit sign in Germany

All the signs in this chapter illustrate three important points:

1. Some of the visual rules, such as those found in European signage, must be understood in order to prevent sending erroneous messages by inadvertently using a significant shape or color. This is especially true since the symbols wind up being used for applications other than just roads. In figure 4-10, classic European road signs are used to indicate whether a pedestrian should "Proceed" or "Do Not Enter" an escalator. Note that the instructions are also communicated visually.

Photographs copyright© 1995 by Tony Fernandes

Figure 4-10 Escalator signs

2. Interface designers are influenced by their environment. American designers need to be aware that other parts of the world are much more used to dealing with visual language on a daily basis.

3. Standards for visual design exist in certain parts of the world.

Design Rule 4: Translate visual components of the target language

As discussed above, visual language is part of everyday life. When designing a user interface, special care must be given to the visual elements. They, along with the text, create the first line of communication with the user. International issues impact the visual design of a product in several ways.

Design for the appropriate reading direction

People take in visual imagery in the same direction they read. For a western reader, the set of images in the dialog box shown in figure 4-11 is read (1)key, (2)connect, (3)entering America Online. This is because English is read from left to right. To an Arabic person that reads from right to left, the images would be read; (3)in America Online, (2)connecting, (1)key. Any design that assumes all users will read images starting from the left will have problems in the Middle East. In addition to images, controls such as progress indicators should be move from right to left for the same reasons .

Discussions of aesthetic issues take place in the "Cultural Aesthetics" chapter.

Note that the numbers in figure 4-11 are not part of the actual product. They were added to aid this discussion.

Figure 4-11 Dialog box from America Online Courtesy of America Online

Lotus 1-2-3 for Windows Arabic is an example of how icon imagery can be changed to match the reading direction of the user. Figure 4-12(a) shows an icon for the original English version of the product. Figure 4-12(b) shows an icon from the Arabic version. Note that the arrowhead should change sides in order to communicate the same idea to somebody reading right to left.

(a)   (b)

Figure 4-12 Arrows Courtesy of Lotus Development Corp.

! ***If you are creating an interface for a right-to-left audience, literally look at your interface in the mirror to get an idea of the way things should look.***

Do not use visual puns. Do use processes.

One of the surefire ways of getting in trouble with visual language is when you use visual puns, i.e. icons that represent an English word or phrase visually. Take a look at figure 4-13. What do you think this sign represents?

Photographs copyright© 1995 by Tony Fernandes

Figure 4-13 2P or not 2P

It turns out that this sign is used in Fort Worth, Texas bars to indicate where the bathroom is: "to pee" go this way. Clearly, this is a sign that will not work internationally because the same expression does not sound like the words for the number 2 nor P in other languages. This type of pun can be found in user interfaces. If an icon begins to enter the realm of "cute," it usually means that it contains an image that will not work internationally. In order for an icon to work around the world, it must represent a process, albeit an abstract one, or an internationally recognized object. For example, the sign in figure 2-14 does a great job of communicating the location of a water fountain by showing the process of drinking.

Photographs copyright© 1995 by Tony Fernandes

Figure 4-14 Water fountain at the Smithsonian, Washington, DC

The sign shows a process with a minimal amount of detail. It represents the bare elements of the process with no national or cultural character.

As these examples illustrate, visual messages can be made to work internationally or they can be hopelessly married to one language. In the Mac version of Macromedia Director's help system, shown in figure 4-15(a), you see an icon with a key on it to represent a "keyword" search. The notion of keywords does not necessarily involve the word "key" in other languages. For example, it could be "main words" in some countries. What would the key have to do with it then? The action being performed is a search and this icon has no hope of conveying that to an international audience.

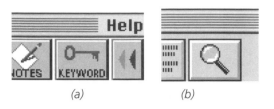

(a)   *(b)*

Figure 4-15 Action is key Courtesy of Macromedia and Claris respectively

The icon in figure 4-15(b) has a much better chance. It focuses on the action of searching. The lens, an object that is used worldwide, is used to convey the message of "looking at things more closely."

The icons shown in figure 4-16(a) are from Lotus 1-2-3 for Windows. The second icon, with somebody running, is intended to let you "run" a macro. The problem is that not everyone "runs" a macro. In France, for example, the metaphor isn't running a macro, it's "throwing" a macro. So the image of somebody running makes absolutely no sense for that locale. The person walking is intended to let you "step" through a macro. It fails for the same reasons.

(a)   *(b)*

This type of symbolism sometimes relies on colors to make it work. In black and white, even Americans would have a hard time understanding it.

Figure 4-16 Stepping and running macros from Lotus 1-2-3 and Microsoft Excel
Courtesy of Lotus and Microsoft respectively

A better solution for international use is to provide an icon that is more abstract. For example, the equivalent icons in Microsoft Excel shown in figure 4-16(b) represent an abstract process and use international tape recorder symbols for play and step.

Figure 4-17(a) shows an icon from Lotus 1-2-3 that translates files. It is trying to communicate this fact by using an icon that represents the notion of going from "apples to oranges"– a very applicable expression, in English, that is.

(a)   *(b)*

Figure 4-17 Lotus and Claris translation icons
Courtesy of Lotus and Claris respectively

A better icon would show some notion of a process, as does the icon for a Claris translator shown in figure 4-17(b).

In the Mac operating system, access to network servers is gained by clicking on the icon shown in figure 4-18. The icon represents a waiter, or "server," with file and folders on his or her tray. Technical terms like server, however, often are not translated from English. Rather, the English word is added to the language. For example, a server is called a "server" in Germany. Unfortunately, the word no longer carries any meaning with it: it is just a technical term whose origin is not understood. This icon, therefore, does not work internationally. A visual representation of a network or other computers would be much better.

Figure 4-18 Mac "server" icon
Courtesy of Apple Computer

Don't use puns in the user interface. They will not work internationally.

The bottom line is, use icons that look like the real object or represent a real process. This doesn't mean that you should produce dry, humorless icons: "fun" icons quite often add life to a design. The message here is that if you do use humor, be prepared to produce another set that works internationally or for other specific target countries. On some occasions, producing multiple sets is the only way to deal with certain situations. For example, B, I, U are commonly used in English versions of products to represent Bolding, Italicizing, and Underlining. They have become a de facto standard of sorts. Of course, those same actions don't start with the same letter in another language. One approach, as used in Claris products, is to provide the BIU for English language products and another set for other Roman script languages, as shown in figure 4-19.

Figure 4-19 Text icons for US and international versions
Courtesy of Claris

I recently saw a product that had an icon of a little table, with four legs, to indicate, you guessed it, that a table of numbers was available. Another was an icon of a wooden log to represent a log file. This stuff just doesn't work in other languages.

Clipart is often a big source of visual misunderstandings. Some examples from Microsoft Powerpoint illustrate this point. Somebody who is not familiar with the meaning of this expression "Under my thumb" would have a difficult time with figure 4-20 since this image does not communicate control as much as a crushing force.

Not everyone would associate the image in figure 4-21 with dealing with several pressures simultaneously. This is a visual rendition of "walking the tightrope."

Another common image is to use the lightbulb to indicate an idea, as shown in figure 4-22. Having an idea is a very elightening thing but the symbol associated with it in the US, the light bulb, is not understood internationally.

Figure 4-20 "Under your thumb" or "crush your head"?
Courtesy of Microsoft

Figure 4-21 Walking the tightrope
Courtesy of Microsoft

Figure 4-22 Having a light bulb?
Courtesy of Microsoft

Note that the light bulb was listed as an object that is recognized internationally in Chapter 2. It is important to draw a distinction between the object and applying meaning to it. The meaning is where the problem is.

Don't bring expressions or humor to life visually. !

Remove text from images

If you are creating an image that shows text and replacing images from locale to locale when not practical, then no discernible text should appear in icons and samples. One approach is to use what is popularly called "greeking". These are meaningless words that appear to be Latin text but in fact say nothing. This is typically found in marketing material, packaging, and on the splash screens of products. A sample of this type of text is shown in figure 4-23.

Lorem ipsum dolor sit amet, consectetuer adipiscing elit, sed diam nonummy nibh euismod tincidunt ut laoreet dolore magna aliquam erat volutpat. Ut wisi enim ad minim veniam, quis nostrud exerci tation ullamcorper suscipit lobortis nisl ut aliquip ex ea commodo consequat. Duis autem vel eum iriure dolor in hendrerit in vulputate velit esse molestie consequat, vel illum dolore eu feugiat nulla facilisis at vero eros et accumsan et iusto odio dignissim qui blandit praesent luptatum zzril delenit augue duis dolore te feugait nulla facilisi.

Figure 4-23 Lorem ipsum used for "greeking"

Another approach is to create the impression of text without showing it. Figure 4-24 shows an example of how this is done. In this

Note that *"left to right"* text is still implied.

example from ClarisWorks, the evolution of a newsletter image is shown. In version 1, figure 4-24(a), the image is drawn in English. In order to provide a localized version, version 2 was created the English was removed and patterns were introduced. Version 2, figure 4-24(b), was ruled out since the patterns appeared Arabic/Hebrew in nature. In order to make sure nobody was offended, version 3, figure 4-24(c), was created with fewer distinct shapes.

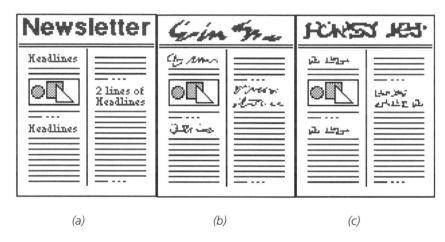

(a)   (b)   (c)

Figure 4-24   Creating a language-neutral image
Courtesy of Claris

One of the classic GUI controls is the checkbox. The user is supposed to check, or put a crossed line, in the square associated with what they want, shown in figure 4-25.

☒ **Hidden Text**
☐ **Table Gridlines**

Figure 4-25 Selecting by crossing

In fact, this convention can cause problems. In as disparate regions of the world as Switzerland and Korea, people select what they want in a form by crossing out what they don't want with an X . Figure 4-26 illustrates how somebody with this approach would indicate the answer "No."

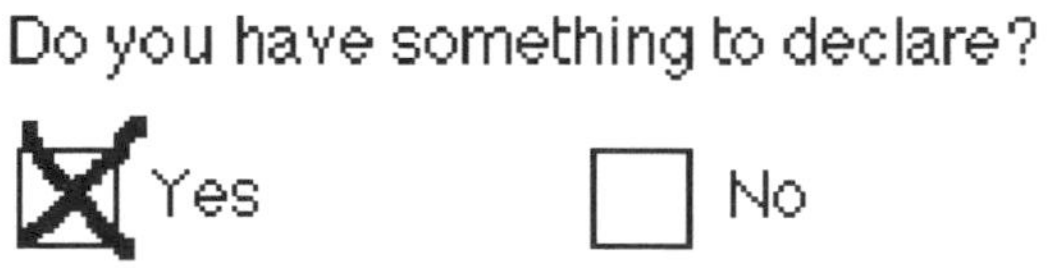
Do you have something to declare?
Yes
No

Figure 4-26 The answer is no

Given this fact, novice spreadsheet users in Europe have trouble with the classic OK and Cancel controls on the entry line(figure 4-27).

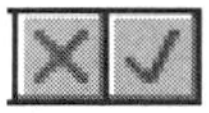

Figure 4-27 OK and Cancel in the Microsoft Excel entry bar
Courtesy of Microsoft

People are tempted to press the X since it is typically used to mark what you want.

National Formats

Written language varies in many ways, yet it always serves the purpose of communicating words and ideas. Some of those ideas are communicated using set orders, set layouts, and a specific set of content. This is formatted information. Formats are interesting because they are independent of language: They are truly a national localization issue. For example, English-speaking countries vary in format standards such as currency and time formats. Formats are an artifact of the locale. In order to produce national localization, the correct formats must be addressed in the user interface.

Design Rule 5: Support native formats

The formatting and content of information is an integral part of many user interfaces. Quite often, software enables users to deal with numbers, measures of time, measures of distance, and complex organizations of information such as street addresses. Formats must be supported by both entry and display in regards to computer software. This is an example of why it is absolutely critical to begin the design process with a list of target countries. Quite often, assumptions regarding formats can break many localizing efforts. By understanding the variations ahead of time, there is a greater opportunity to develop a reasonable base design.

Numbers

Although the notion of numbers is universal, there are many different ways to represent values. These differences can be problematic in any parts of the interface that allow for the input, or representation, of numbers. Intelligent handling of number formatting, like putting a comma in the right place, will have to be changed for each locale. Table 5-1 shows number formats and table 5-2 shows ordinal values from some countries around the world. As you can see, punctuation assumptions cannot be made.

Number	Country of Usage
1 234,56	Finland, France, Luxembourg, Portugal, Sweden,
1.234,56	Albania, Argentina, Belgium, Czechoslovakia, Denmark, Greece, Holland, Hungary, Germany, Ireland, Italy, Spain, others
1.234 56	Russia
1,23456	Japan
1'234.56	Switzerland
1,234.56	US, Canada, China

Table 5-1 Floating point numbers

Number	Country of Usage
1,2,3,4...	Austria, Germany, Scandinavia, Switzerland(German), others
1°,2°,3°,4°...	Italy, Portugal, Spain, Switzerland(Italian)
1ste,2de,3de,4de...	Belgium, Netherlands
1st,2nd,3rd,4th...	US, Canada(English), Ireland, UK

Table 5-2 Ordinal numbers

Figure 5-1 shows the Macintosh control panel that allows the user to set the default number format. What makes this a great design is that the particular details of the format can be overridden in order to accommodate regional variations.

! **Make sure your interface doesn't make assumptions about the punctuation used with numbers.**

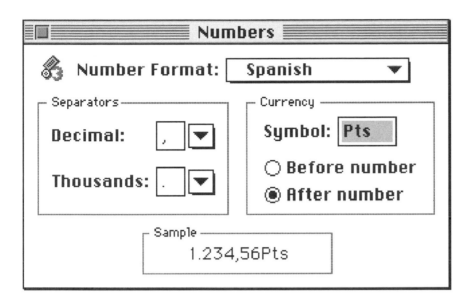

Figure 5-1 The Mac numbers control panel Courtesy of Apple Computer

Currency

Currency not only varies because of the symbol and number formats, it also varies by the placement of the symbol. The variations are so great that only a few countries are shown in table 5-3. A financial institution native to the target locales should be consulted for a complete list.

Symbols	Example	Country of Usage
DM	DM 1,23 DM 1,- 1,23 DM	Germany
L. ,Lit	Lit 123 LIT 123 L 123 L. 123	Italy
F, FF, c, ct, cs	12F34 FF 1.23 1,23 F 1,23 FF F 1,23	France
Esc., $	1$23 Esc. 1.23	Portugal

Symbols	Example	Country of Usage(cont.)
Kr, kr, -:, :-	-:50	Sweden
	50:-	
	Kr 12:-	
	12 Kr	
	1,23 kr	
£, p	123p	United Kingdom
	£1.23	
	GB£1.23	
$, ¢	34¢	United States
	.34	
	$12	
	$12.34	

Table 5-3 Currency

Currency formats not only vary from country to country, they also vary slightly within the country. The best way to handle this is by giving the user a set of formats, as shown in figure 5-2.

Excel reads the correct currency format from the operating system settings. When applications do this, it makes it easier for users because they only have to describe the format once for all their applications.

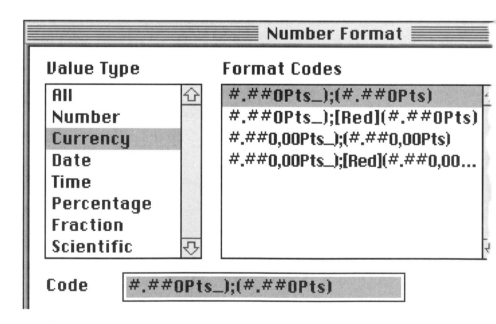

Figure 5-2 Microsoft Excel currency formatting dialog box Courtesy of Microsoft

In Microsoft Windows, figure 5-3, the user is allowed control over the placement of the symbol as well as the symbol used. This control enables a user to work with currency formats independently of the interface's language and to allow for local variations in placement. The ability to type in the currency symbol allows people to specify currencies that may not be supported by the operating system.

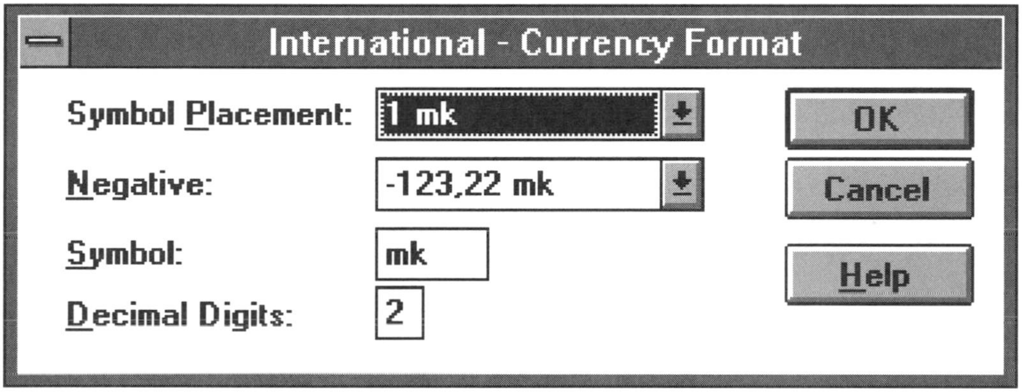

Figure 5-3 Currency dialog box from Microsoft Windows Courtesy of Microsoft

Support multiple currency formats in the interface. Most overseas companies need to conduct business in a variety of currencies.

Calendars

People can't even agree on how to measure years. There is the classic Gregorian calendar, which is used by most Western countries. There is also the Arabic lunar calendar, used in many Arabic countries. There's the Jewish calendar, there's the Iranian calendar, and there's the Japanese imperial calendar. Think of the assumptions that may be made about the calculation of dates, holidays, etc., that can become totally null and void as the product moves from country to country. If the product deals with tracking business transactions and it will be shipped in Japan, you have to seriously consider supporting the imperial calendar as well as the Gregorian calendar.

The imperial calendar will enable your product to be used in traditional Japanese businesses that still track time by the year of the emperor's reign, and the Gregorian calendar will be used by more progressive firms as well as those that do business in the United States and Europe. In providing this functionality, make sure you do it in the right way. Lotus implemented support for the imperial calendar in 1-2-3. They thought they were doing their customers a favor by having a feature that reset the calendar to zero. This would save their customers a trip to the store, should the emperor pass away. The feature was viewed as being very negative because it implied that the emperor was not immortal. The feature was removed. At the very least, you should give your users the ability to use the typical date formats. Figure 5-4 shows a popup from ClarisImpact-J that allows the user to select a Gregorian date written in Japanese, an imperial date, or a Gregorian date in English.

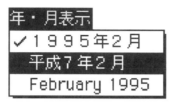

Figure 5-4 "2nd month of 7th year" Courtesy of Claris

Holidays complicate things greatly because they change as soon as you cross the border. In MeetingMaker, a calendar-based meeting scheduler by On Technologies, there is a great feature that flags holidays. You can look over the year and easily spot an upcoming holiday, as shown in figure 5-5.

Another problem with scheduling products is dealing with time zones. If you schedule a meeting, the product must be able to adjust the appointment time according to all the users native time zones.

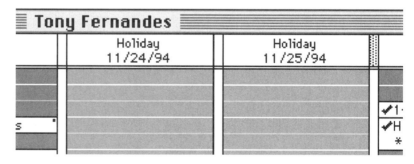

Figure 5-5 MeetingMaker Courtesy of On Technologies

The problem is, if you were using this feature to guide your delivery schedule in Europe, you would run into situations where you tried to deliver products during somebody's holiday. For the European market, you should be allowed to view other countries' holidays. Calendar features, in particular, must be designed with international issues in mind from the beginning or else it will be very difficult to make them useful for international users.

In addition to the varieties of calendar types, the appearance of each of those calendar types varies from locale to locale. The Gregorian calendars in the US are typically presented with Sunday as the first day. European calendars, on the other hand, typically start on Monday.

Although Europe uses the same calendar, the days and months are written differently because of the variations in language. Table 5-4 shows the spelling differences of the 12 months in several European languages.

Months	Abbrev.	Country of Usage
janvier	jan.	France
février	fév.	
mars	mar.	
avril	avr.	
mai	mai	
juin	juin	
juillet	juil.	
août	aoû.	
septembre	sep.	
octobre	oct.	
novembre	nov.	
décembre	déc.	
Januar	Jan	Germany, Austria, Switzerland(German)
Februar	Feb	
März	Mär	
April	Apr	
Mai	Mai	
Juni	Jun	
Juli	Jul	
August	Aug	
September	Sep	
Oktober	Okt	
November	Nov	
Dezember	Dez	
januari	jan	Sweden
februari	feb	
mars	mar	
april	apr	
maj	maj	

Although the spelling of the months is the same, the abbreviations used in French-speaking Switzerland are different from those used in France. For example, January is abbreviated janv. This is a prime example why formats need to be looked at as national issues rather than as language issues.

Months	Abbrev.	Country of Usage(cont.)
juli	*juli*	
augusti	*aug*	
september	*sept*	
oktober	*okt*	
november	*nov*	
december	*dec*	
juni	*juni*	
January	*Jan*	*US, UK*
February	*Feb*	
March	*Mar*	
April	*Apr*	
May	*May*	
June	*Jun*	
July	*Jul*	
August	*Aug*	
September	*Sep*	
October	*Oct*	
November	*Nov*	
December	*Dec*	

Note that some countries use multiple formats and will therefore appear several times in a given table.

Notice how words can generate different meanings in other languages. The abbreviation for the word "Friday" in Portuguese is "Sex".

Table 5-4 Months

Making assumptions about the number of letters that an abbreviated day takes is sure to cause you problems. Notice that the abbreviations for months in table 5-4 ranged from three to four characters. In order to handle days and months correctly, variable-length abbreviations must be supported. For example, producing a calendar in Microsoft Publisher in Portuguese (figure 5-6) produced three-letter abbreviations, and the same calendar done in German (figure 5-7) produced two-character abbreviations.

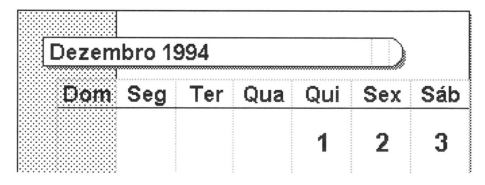

Figure 5-6 Portuguese calendar from Microsoft Publisher Courtesy of Microsoft

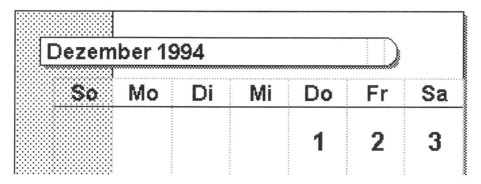

Figure 5-7 French calendar from Microsoft Publisher

Dates

As time changes the world, the world changes time. The way a user specifies a date in various parts of the world represents many permutations of month, day, and year ordering. Table 5-5 gives a sample of the short form of dates:

Both of these calendars blew it in one respect: In Europe, the first day of the week in a calendar is typically Monday.

Date	Country of Usage
31.1.95	Austria, Belgium, Canada, Finland, Germany, Ireland, Italy, Netherlands, Norway, Portugal, UK
31-1-95	Belgium, Canada, Netherlands
31.01.95	France, Germany, Norway, Portugal
31. 1. '95	Iceland
95/1/31	Arabia
95-1-31	Sweden
1/31/95	US

Table 5-5 Short form of dates

Because the long form of dates involves written words, the variations for dates are greater. Table 5-6 shows a very brief sample.

Date	Country of Usage
ut 31. le 1995	Czechoslovakia
1995. jan. 31., kedd	Hungary
wto, 31 sty, 1995	Poland
31. tammikuuta 1995	Finland
31. Januar 1995	Germany
31 Gennaio 1995	Italy
Tue, Jan 31, 1995	US

Table 5-6 Long form of dates

61

As shown in figure 5-8, the Mac operating system handles the problems of date by letting the user select the date format by country. In addition, the user is allowed to select the order of items for both the long and short versions of the date. This will take into account multiple formats within the borders of a single country.

Days of the week are spelled differently and they are of course abbreviated differently. In particular, be aware that abbreviations exist using the Roman alphabet as well as other scripts. The design must support all the appropropriate abbreviations. For example, in figure 5-8, this ClarisImpact-J dialog box offers the user the ability to choose from three English and two Japanese ways of displaying the days of the week.

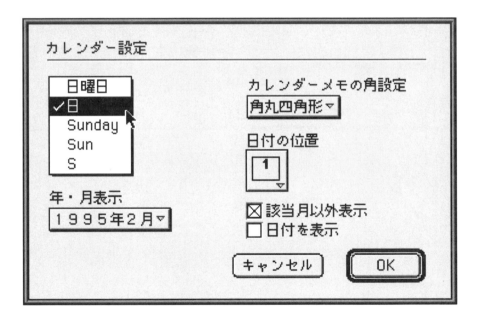

Figure 5-8 Day of the week selection in ClarisImpact J Courtesy of Claris

Time

Time stands still for no person. Time formatting doesn't stand still as one goes around the globe either. The US and Canada use the a.m./p.m. system, which stands for ante meridian, post meridian. Much of Europe is on a 24- hour clock. One o'clock in the afternoon in the US would be thirteen hours in Europe. This is known in the US as military time. This difference is only one of many that can be found in the way the world tells time, as shown in table 5-7.

Morning	Afternoon	Country of Usage
10:00 Uhr	14:00 Uhr	Austria, Germany
10:00	14:00	Denmark, Spain, UK
10.00	14.00	Finland, Germany, Italy, Netherlands
kl 10.00kl	14.00	Norway, Sweden
10:00 du.	2:00 de.	Hungary
10:00 AM	2:00 PM	US

Table 5-7 Time formats

On the Mac, time formats can be set by selecting a country, as shown in figure 5-9. Similarly, in Microsoft Windows, selecting a location will set the time format for you. As shown in figure 5-10, the interface allows you to have control over whether the time has a leading 0 or not, as well as control over the separator to deal with local variations.

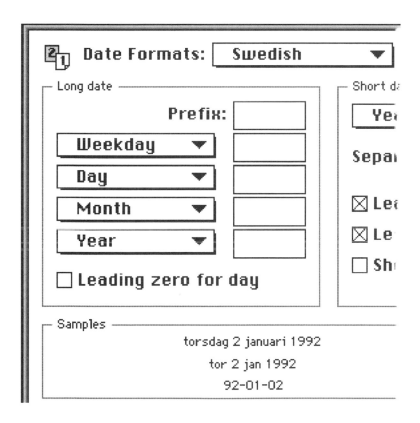

Figure 5-9 Mac date format dialog box Courtesy of Apple Computer

Figure 5-10 Time dialog box from Microsoft Windows Courtesy of Microsoft

! *Time is of the essence. Make sure that you not only support the right format, but allow for multiple sets of holidays in locales that have many countries close together.*

Units of measure

The US and Canada use the English system of measurement, and most of the world uses the metric system; it's as simple as that. In addition to the difference in input, units can impact a user interface if the product ships with clipart or other predone material that was created with inches and is then run on a machine using centimeters. The art does not automatically convert and you wind up with very strange-looking clipart indeed.

Postal addresses

Postal addresses may vary in terms of the order of the names, the order of all the text in general, and how numbers are used. You need to make sure that you supply enough fields for all the elements and an additional line for the country that it will ship to. Table 5-8 shows some examples.

Address	*Country of Usage*
A l'attention de: Melanie Evian Information Parisienne 45, Rue des Deportees F-80100 Amiens France	France
Juni Gmbh z.H. Hermann Schmidt Friedrich-List Strasse 13a D-8500 Nuernberg 42 Deutchland	Germany
Senhor Antonio Manuel Simões Fernandes Pedra Avenida de Saõ Jorge, n°12 L-1000 Coimbra Portugál	Portugal
Nippon Institute Attn: MS. Yomata 1-56 Ichigaya-daimachi Shinjuku-ku, Tokyo 156 Japan	Japan
Claris Corporation Attn: Human Experience Group 5201 Patrick Henry Drive Santa Clara, CA 95125 USA	US

Table 5-8 Postal addresses

In user interfaces, addresses can be very tricky. The most common trap is to create fixed fields in a fixed order in the interface. Another common problem is to not allow enough fields to support the inclusion of a country specification. In Lotus Ami 2.0, there is a dialog box that lets the user enter addresses for a phone and address book (figure 5-11). Not only does the dialog box contain some fields that only correspond to the US and Canada, it presents them in order only suitable for the US and Canada. In addition, note that there is no field for country. This interface assumes that you will never be writing to people in other countries.

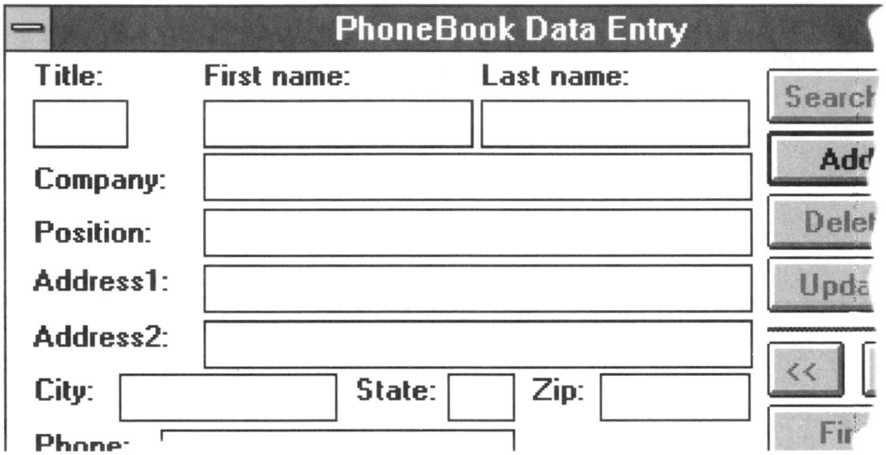

Figure 5-11 Lotus Ami Pro address entry Courtesy of Lotus Development Corp.

One way of dealing with this problem is to change the interface for every country. Another is to present users with a generic set of fields that can be filled in with whatever makes sense. Microsoft Works uses the latter method, as shown in figure 5-12. This particular design works well except for the fact that only four lines are allowed. An international address that includes a company name will typically need five lines.

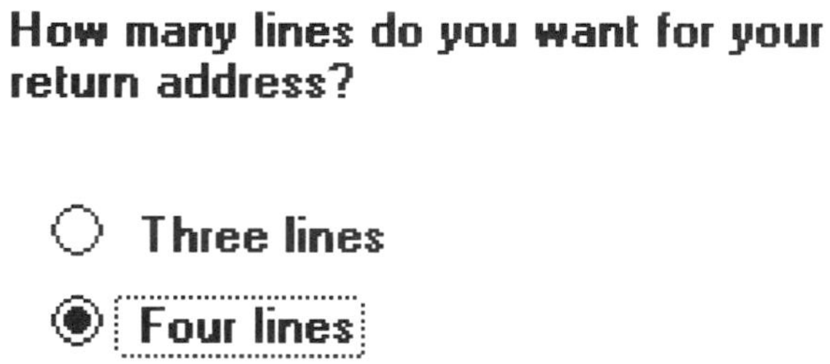

Figure 5-12 MicrosoftWorks address entry Courtesy of Microsoft

Telephone numbers

The world may be a phone call away but the number you dial changes in structure from country to country. Table 5-9 give a brief look at some of the variations found in Europe.

Phone number	Country of Usage
1234 56 78 90	Austria
12-345 67 89	Belgium
12 34 56 78	Denmark
(123)4 56 78 90	Germany
(12)3456789	Italy
123-456 78 90	Portugal
123-45-6-789-0000	Japan
(800)123-4567	US

Table 5-9 Telephone numbers

An easy way of handling phone numbers is to provide an unformatted line to allow users to type in whatever number they like. An example of this technique, as it is used in Claris Organizer, is shown in figure 5-13. These controls appear in a dialog box and put no restriction on the placement of parenthesis, etc. Figure 5-14 shows how controls could be designed to make life easy for US customers but difficult for everyone else.

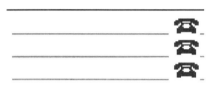

Figure 5-13 ClarisOrganizer telephone number entry Courtesy of Claris

Figure 5-14 Formatted entry

Other National Conventions

Be aware that various items have national standards applied to them. If your product contains one of these, it will almost certainly mean that material will have to be redone. For example, flow chart symbols in the US usually conform to ANSI standards. These standards dictate the shape and proportion of the symbols. In Germany, flow chart symbols are designed according to DIN standards. Color specification standards, such as Pantone, in the US, have equivalents in other countries of such as Japan where Toyo is used.

Inform yourself about all the standards that apply to your design. **!**

6   *The Physical World*

What good is running if you are on the wrong road?
German

A person assesses whether a place is familiar or not by looking at the environmental colors, textures, and shapes. It should be the goal of all user interface designers to make the experience of using a software product as comfortable and familiar as possible. One solution is to make the experience of the real world and the look and feel of the computer seamless. There's only one problem: the look and feel of the world varies from place to place. As you can see from figures 6-1 through 6-4, places vary in color, style, and texture. Everyday objects vary in the same way.

Photographs copyright© 1995 by Tony Fernandes

Figure 6-1 Northern California

Photographs copyright© 1995 by Tony Fernandes

Figure 6-2 Brussels, Belgium

Photographs copyright© 1995 by Tony Fernandes

Figure 6-3 Osaka, Japan

Photographs copyright© 1995 by Tony Fernandes

Figure 6-4 Coimbra, Portugal

When one reads a classic interface design book, one of the techniques that is invariably mentioned is the use of metaphor. Metaphor, some books say, enables users to "bring knowledge of the real world to the computer." On the surface that sounds reasonable. The problem is that there is more than one real world that the user interface could be based on. As a designer, it is important to understand that today's interfaces have been unnaturally influenced by the American environment, in particular the American office. The "real world" elements contained within them are mostly American realities. Why? Because designers and developers drew upon the world around them for ideas. For the US, the use of metaphor has worked reasonably well. If it is to work as well in other parts of the world, designers must be open to rethinking the notion of metaphor for different locales.

Even if a metaphor was found to be applicable, there is always the problem of objects used within the metaphor. Common everyday objects are just not the same everywhere. The presence or lack of certain objects may create the feeling of unfamiliarity, a feeling that all interfaces should be trying to avoid. This chapter will discuss the issue of enhancing usability by ridding the interface of unfamiliar objects.

In order to produce a good interface design, designers must understand their target user. Users are greatly affected by their environment. Therefore, to develop a successful design, designers need to understand their users' environment and take it into account as part of the national localization process.

Even a natural phenomenon can be unfamiliar. Ajax had to change its advertising campaign overseas because nobody knew what a "white tornado" was: The white tornado was the symbol for the product in the US.

Design Rule 6: Use appropriate and familiar objects

Just by looking around you as you read this book, you will see everyday objects: objects that provide design inspiration but also objects that may be different in other parts of the world. Of these, there are some objects in particular that are relevant to software and user interfaces.

Paper sizes

Paper sizes vary. In the US, the most common paper size is 8 1/2 by 11. In Europe and Japan A4 is most often used. On a secondary level, legal sized paper is used in the US quite a bit. In Europe and Japan, B5 is used. As you can see in figure 6-5, the differences are greater than just the name. The sheets are different sizes.

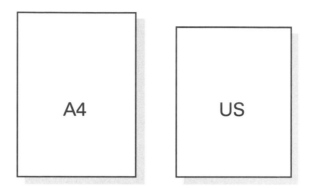

Figure 6-5 A4 vs US letter

The differences extend to envelopes as well. The standard North American business envelope is 105 mm by 241 mm. The standard European envelopes are DL envelopes that measure 162 mm by 229 mm and C5 envelopes that measure 110 mm by 220 mm.

These differences are significant in the following ways:

- If the interface presents the user with a blank page, as is commonly done in word processors and graphics products, the correct default paper size should be presented according to locale.

- Any predone material such as samples cannot assume a single paper size.

- These differences in shape contribute to the user's sense of familiarity. Therefore, icons that represent sheets of paper should be correctly proportioned for the locale.

- Any transmitted material, such as faxes, will have to be designed to make sure they fit properly in the typical paper sizes of the target countries.

One way of dealing with this issue in the interface is by giving the user a choice of page sizes. This is done in ClarisImpact from Claris Corporation, as shown in figure 6-6. When users create a presentation, they are given the opportunity to select the media it will be shown or printed on. Once the selection is made, the slide background provided adjusts itself to the selection. This not only allows the interface to work all over the world, it also allows a user to create a presentation in another size for use in another locale.

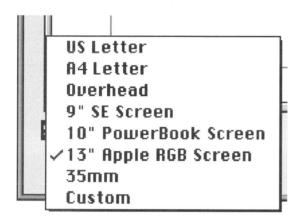

Figure 6-6 ClarisImpact media selector Courtesy of Claris

Another approach is to let the user select the page size from the standard operating system "page setup" dialog box an example of which is shown in figure 6-7.

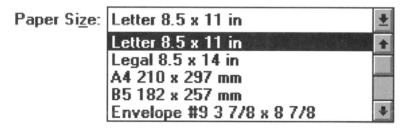

Figure 6-7 Page size selection from Microsoft Windows Courtesy of Microsoft

Keep paper sizes in mind when creating any applications that print out material directly or indirectly. An example of indirect printing is faxing. Yes, fax paper sizes vary to match the countries standard paper sizes.

No matter what, the product must support the creation of material targeted at different paper sizes. **!**

Mailboxes

Things like mailboxes are very different all over the world, and you can't make any assumptions about what people will look at and understand as a mailbox. Nevertheless, icons appear in user interfaces that display the US bias, as shown in figure 6-8 and 6-9.

Figure 6-8 The US rural mailbox and selectPHONE mail icon
Courtesy of Pro CD

Figure 6-9 The US mailbox and an icon from Internet Express
Courtesy of Phoenix Technologies

In other parts of the world, what is thought of as a mailbox has a very different look, as shown in figures 6-10 and 6-11.

Figure 6-10 Dutch mailbox

Figure 6-11 Japanese mailbox

Initial users of the Mac in the UK thought that the trash can was a mailbox. The Japanese mailbox looks like a US trash can as well.

When dealing with mail, the best approach is to stay away from where the mail goes and comes from. Instead, concentrate on what the mail looks like. The appearance of an envelope is something that is recognizable around the world. It is also a simple shape that lends itself well to icons, as shown in figure 6-12.

Figure 6-12 Mail icons from Timbuktu, AOL, and CC:Mail
Courtest of Farallon, America Online, and Lotus

Telephones

Like mailboxes, telephones vary in shape and configuration, as shown in figure 6-13. The phone booths they can be found in vary equally in look as well, as shown in figure 6-14.

Photographs copyright© 1995 by Tony Fernandes

Figure 6-13 Japanese telephone

Photographs copyright© 1995 by Tony Fernandes

Figure 6-14 Dutch telephone booth

In addition to shapes, phones often have colors associated with them. In the US, blue is often used to indicate telephones because of the AT&T legacy. In Japan and the Netherlands, green is often used for telephones.

Keyboard layouts are not standard. For example, Norwegian telephones have the number 1 in the bottom left-hand corner. A standard layout shown in figure 6-15 would not work in every country.

Figure 6-15 The Apple Phone layout
Courtesy of Apple Computer

When dealing with telephones, the most recognizable image to use is of the handset: That shape is used all over the world. Beyond the headset, use images of very common configurations. Some images that will work well internationally are shown in figure 6-16.

Figure 6-16 Apple Phone, Windows Terminal, and Lotus Organizer Directory
Courtesy of Apple, Microsoft, and Lotus

Office supplies

Since many user interfaces are created for, and invented in, offices they contain many artifacts from that environment. As figures 6-17 through 6-19 show, the American office has gotten into user interfaces.

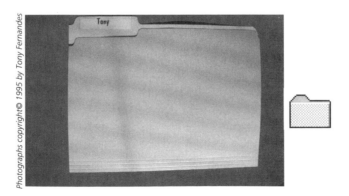

Photographs copyright© 1995 by Tony Fernandes

Figure 6-17 Folders Icon courtesy of Apple Computer

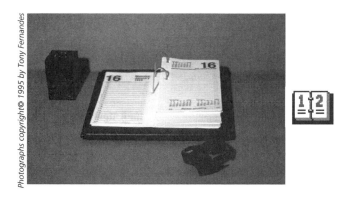

Figure 6-18 Calendars   *Icon courtesy of Microsoft*

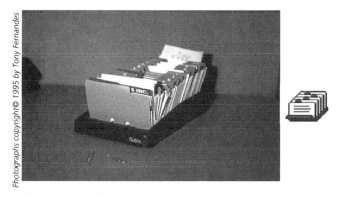

Figure 6-19 Rolodex *Icon courtesy of Microsoft*

Figure 6-20 shows these and other examples of artifacts that can be problematic. Some problems with these icons include:

- Not every office has a flipbook-type calendar.

- Rolodex-type devices are not used all over the world.

- Folders with raised tabs are not used universally.

- The metaphor of a clipboard is not applicable everywhere. Other metaphors are used to convey the idea of an intermediate media. Cut & paste, does not have the same connotation in certain parts of the world. The clipboard may not be something that's even understood or used.

- Metal trash cans with a lid are not used in every country.

- File cabinets vary in design and configuration

Figure 6-20 Bits and pieces of the American reality
Courtesy (clockwise from to right) Microsoft, Apple, Microsoft, Microsoft, Microsoft, Microsoft, Microsoft, Apple

! *When you look for inspiration for your icons, get inspired in your target locales, not your office.*

Text orientation

Because text is such a large part of user interfaces, it is important to be sure that it is presented correctly. European languages are written from left to right. Arabic and Hebrew are written right to left, etc. In addition, however, you must be aware of the context the text is being used in. For example, it is a popular idea to use books or tabbed notebooks as a metaphor for applications. As was discussed earlier in this book, the pages may naturally turn from right to left. An additional issue that can make a book look unnatural is the orientation of the text along the spine. In the US, the text typically flows from top to bottom. In Germany and France, and a lot of other foreign countries, the text flows from the bottom to the top. A sample of each orientation for the same magazine is shown in figure 6-21.

The world outside the office

In addition to office artifacts, many other conventions and attributes of the environment must be recognized, understood, and handled correctly in software. This is particularly relevant to multimedia applications and any interface that draws upon the world found

Figure 6-21 Text orientation

outdoors. For example, can you spot the items in figure 6-22 that create a non-Japanese sense of place in the "Just Grandma & Me" CD-ROM from Living Books?

Some of them are easy...

- The mailbox is not typical.
- The bus says "Beach" in English.

Slightly more difficult to spot are...

- The yellow school bus is not typical outside North America.
- The clothing is not typical.
- The white picket fence is not typical.
- The open spaces and architecture are not typical.

Difficult to spot ...

- The bus should drive along the right side of the road.
- The bear should be driving from the left side of the bus.
- The door should be on the other side of the bus.
- They should be waiting on the other side of the road because that's where the door would be.

Given all this, this product presents a story of North Americans going on a trip, certainly not Japanese characters going on a trip.

Figure 6-22 Just Grand Ma and me Courtesy of Broderbund

Signs

Another item found in the outside world is signs. In order to create a sense of place, any electronic representation of the outdoors must take signs into account. Signs are one of the everyday objects encountered by people and designers. Like everything else, they creep into the user interfaces with a US bias, as shown in figure 6-23 and 6-24.

Figure 6-23 Merge from road and from Lotus Ami Pro
Icon courtesy of Lotus Development Corp.

Traffic signs are certainly artifacts that contribute to sense of place. As shown in figure 6-24, they can give the viewer some immediate clues about where they are. In this case, the signs are from Japan and Germany, respectively.

Figure 6-24 Signs in Japan and Germany

Beyond roadside applications, signs create a sense of place because they embody certain styles and character. For example, US signs are all over the map, not only in terms of color but also typography, as shown in figure 6-25.

Figure 6-25 American signs with an informal touch

Other countries such as Germany have signs with much more of a recognizable character. They typically use sans serif fonts with a great deal of white space, as shown in figure 6-26.

Figure 6-26 German signs

With signs, the style says a great deal about where it is from and if it belongs. !

Appropriateness

In addition to all the physical differences in the environment, you will have to judge whether all facets of the user interface are appropriate for the typical user's work/entertainment setting. For example, sound queues may add a great deal to your interface but you must look carefully at their impact. In most US office space, people have their own office or cube: There is relative privacy. In some locales such as Japan, you can find offices where six people work around the same desk, with a boss at one end. In this environment, sound could make things rather unpleasant for everyone, especially the user of your product. That is exactly what Lotus found when it shipped Lotus 1-2-3 Release 2.0J. Like the US version, it beeped every time you made an error. It drove people in some Japanese office settings absolutely crazy. It not only annoyed everyone around the computer, worse, it announced to the world that you made a mistake. This made people feel very dishonorable. The beep was quickly made an option in the next release. Even the smallest inappropriate design can have a huge impact on the success of the product.

Color

Colors have symbolic meaning. In the US, red, white, and blue signify patriotism. Orange and black can signify Halloween or caffeinated and decaffeinated coffee. Green and red are associated with the Christmas holiday.

Likewise, colors have symbolic meanings in other parts of the world. Being aware of these meanings can make a huge difference to the success of your design. When EuroDisney set out to design their signs, they wanted to create a color scheme that would rival Coca Cola's red. What they came up with were signs with a great deal of purple[2]. How did they arrive at purple? Eisner, the CEO, liked it. The only problem is that purple symbolizes death in Catholic Europe. More precisely, it symbolizes the crucifixion. Many visitors thought the signs were "morbid," not the kind of reaction Disney intended.

Colors can also represent nationalism and politics. Many political parties represent themselves using colors. The obvious ones are the "Green" parties that are for preserving the environment as opposed to various "Red" parties that are communist. Colors can easily represent nationalism: Flags are a testament to that fact. Using colors from a flag can immediately create an impression in the user's mind. For example, light blue and white might be a sign of patriotism in Israel, a very unpopular combination in Arabic countries, a symbol of patriotism in Greece, and a very unpopular combination in Turkey. Oriental cultures have relatively formal symbolic colors. Red in China is the color of celebration and white is the color of death: people often wear white clothing to a funeral. In the US, however, black is considered the color of mourning and white is associated with weddings.

! *Make sure you pick your colors carefully. Like every other subject in this chapter, ignoring the symbolic meaning may be a costly mistake.*

Introduction to Culture

Previous discussions have presented the differences in language, formats, and in the physical environment. All of these issues are relevant to national localization. Cultural localization deals with how those differences impact people and their behavior. Also, history and values all can impact the user's perception of the user interface. Before discussing how culture impacts the design of software, it's important to first gain an understanding of what culture is. Culture is something in which people take pride. It gives us all a sense of dignity. It must be respected in the user interface.

Culture

The word "culture" is very generic and can sometimes be all encompassing. Culture can exist within an age group, as an artifact of a social class, etc. The discussion in this book will be limited to the notion of "national culture" in which people from a locale have developed similar beliefs, are exposed to similar media, and share a common history.

Culture is defined as the "the collective mental programming of the people in an environment."[3] That being the case, in order to understand people, you need to understand their environment. The previous chapter presented some of the environmental differences that impact people's lives and perception. Culture can be further broken down into four main components[4]: values, rituals, heroes, and symbols. These components are built one on top of the other with values at the very core. Surrounding values are the rituals that reinforce the values, the heroes that are part of the rituals and represent the values, and the symbols that represent all of the above. Culture is significant to user interface design because quite often a design will touch several of these areas consciously or unconsciously. If the interface does not take the cultural symbols, heroes and rituals into account, misunderstandings can result. If an interface insults people's values, the impact can be far worse. Insulting someone's culture intentionally or unintentionally is pure TNT. It may not only prevent somebody from using your product, it may prevent someone from using any of your company's products ever again.

Design Rule 7: Understand your cultural blind spots. Take the culture of the target nations into account.

People are often ethnocentric[5], i.e., they are blinded by their own culture. Designers are no different. As the components of culture are discussed, it is important to begin to recognize where your blind spots might be. Examples from the American experience will be used to illustrate this point.

When learning about other cultures, it is important to suspend judgment. Have an open mind.

Values

When you deal with values, you often deal with issues that people tend to be very intransigent about. Values are very slow to change. When you start dealing with people's values, you start dealing with issues that evoke a great deal of emotion because quite often they have developed over a long period of time.

Values represent a society's belief about what's right and what's wrong, what's evil, what's good, what's clean, what's dirty, what's natural, what's unnatural, what's lawful and unlawful, proper, and improper. It gets down to what people believe in their hearts and minds. You know you are dealing with values when you hear a topic that you know will create disagreement between people. In the American experience, there are some issues that touch the world of values and therefore become lightning rods for disagreement.

- Equality of the sexes
- Racial equality
- Sexuality
- Abortion
- Animal rights
- Taxes
- Nudity
- Guns
- AIDS
- Family values

I just report these things. If you get insulted by anything you read, then you will understand what your user may feel when using your product.

It is important to understand that people have varying sets of values. Some might look at the signs from the US in figure 7-1 and laugh or others might be offended. But because most Americans are aware of the Las Vegas wedding chapels and some of the attractions found in the western United States, they would think that there was nothing unusual about the signs.

Figure 7-1 Some signs from Nevada

A user interface can be impacted by somebody's values in some subtle and not so subtle ways. For example, clipart portraying a woman in a position of power, as shown in figure 7-2, is going to be offensive to cultures that don't subscribe to the notion of gender equality.

Figure 7-2 Not everyone shares the same values
Courtesy of Microsoft

I'm not saying that designers should or should not portray what they believe is right. I am saying the notion of right and wrong varies and so will people's reactions to certain images. Along the same lines, there are countries where polygamy is legal. Designing an interface for names and addresses that assume only one spouse may be problematic.

Men holding hands in the West may be considered a sign of homosexuality. In Arab countries such as Saudi Arabia, it is considered a sign of friendship and honor.

Sex and nudity vary in acceptability. In cultures such as Scandinavia, France, and Japan, sexual images and issues tend to be much more openly dealt with. In Japan, images of condoms and other sexual content can be found in collections of business clipart. Even in the advertising of computer hardware, nudity can be an acceptable component, as shown in figure 7-3.

It's also important to realize that the American culture is unique in some ways. It's unique in the diversity of people, and the diversity of beliefs. Other countries that are much smaller don't have that kind of diversity and typically have belief systems that are much more uniform.

Photographs copyright© 1995 by Tony Fernandes

Figure 7-3 Japanese equipment ad

PowerSoft ran an ad in Denmark with a woman straddling a chair with her legs which read, "Sometimes size isn't important...if you have the right tool." People at the US headquarters were offended by the ad but the Danish office insisted that suggestive ads are just par for the course in that market.

In terms of animal rights, you might imagine how insulting an image of a cat as food might be in the US. A cow as an image of food would be just as insulting to other cultures, although it's accepted here. More on food later.

Imagine software that shows images such as a marijuana leaf that seems to condone the use of drugs. That is exactly the impression people from a country that outlaws alcohol will have when they see an image of alcohol or champagne glasses often used in clipart libraries.

Some English computer terminology has evolved with language that is inappropriate if seen out of context. Problems can occur when the terminology is translated literally. Some of the terminology in this category includes "abort," "drag & drop," and "nuke." Imagine a user in Hiroshima having to press a button that reads "nuke."

Without a thorough knowledge of what a target market's values are, there is a very good chance that designs will be produced that will be offensive to people. Of particular interest are cultural taboos. Taboos are such a broad topic that the next chapter is devoted to them.

Rituals

Rituals are actions taken by people that often reflect and celebrate a culture's values. Rituals include politeness, respect, the work ethic, political processes, sports, problem-solving processes, and even religion.

Note that baseball's championship is called the World Series. In basketball, the champions of the National Basketball League are entitled World Champions. This makes a statement about how oblivious to the existence of other cultures the US can be. In the American experience, typical rituals include:

- Football culminating in the Super Bowl
- Baseball which culminates in the World Series
- National Republican and Democratic conventions
- The shaking of hands
- Expression of opinion
- The nine-to-five (and then some) work ethic
- The "American way"
- Individuality
- Management hierarchies
- Trial and error

Rituals can impact the user interfaces if metaphors are developed that employ a cultural norm as a model. Any design that assumes knowledge of a sport is problematic. Some common American notions that can sometimes creep into products are the "penalty box" from hockey and being "at bat" from baseball.

Rituals can also impact how certain features are presented to the users. For example, a software product that increases productivity is often presented to American users as something that will let them do more. In Europe, the product would be better presented as a way of getting you home earlier. Software that is perceived as fun may be rejected for serious applications because fun and work may not be two things that can be mixed in a culture.

Striving for innovation is quite often synonymous with using the "trial and error" method. Although it is cherished in the US, the thought of failure as part of a process is a lot less desirable to some cultures. In Japan, failure is not acceptable and is thought dishonorable. When Lotus 1-2-3 for DOS was introduced in Japan, it had a lukewarm reception because it beeped every time there was an error condition. Since many Japanese office settings have several people around the same table, the audible beep told everyone else that you were making mistakes: very dishonorable. The beep was made an option in the following release.

The notion of individuality and the expression of opinion, a hallmark of the American experience, is not highly regarded universally. In the US, it is common to say that the "squeaky wheel gets the grease." The implication is that the person who stands out is rewarded. In Japan, the same expression reads "the tallest nail gets hammered first." In this context, the person who stands out gets put it their place. User interfaces, especially those in the groupware category, must be able to deal with varying levels of individuality and anonymity that are required.

Even the act of purchasing is not universal. The American purchasing process can be very confusing. There is a price marked on the product, then quite often there is a sign near it that indicates some percentage will be taken off. When you bring it to the register, the amount is taken off and in many places, a percentage is added on for taxes. You either have to be an arithmetical genius or you just have to take your chances as to whether you're going to have enough money or not, but you certainly don't know down to the penny what you are going to pay. Any user interface that involves shopping must be careful to correctly represent the shopping method of the target country or culture.

In the US, problems are approached in the form of extremes in order to get to yes or no answers. Typically, a meeting begins by individuals presenting their extreme view. For example, "if you don't give me the resources that I need, I will not ship a product by a given date." And someone on the other side of the table might say, "Well, if I give you all these resources, then we're going to go broke." Once everyone presents their extreme case, the negotiation begins. In Europe[3] meetings are typically handled with a much more dialectic approach, in which differences are abolished among people and consensus can be arrived at. The Japanese use a much more holistic approach in which there is an attempt to recognize the overall feeling of the group rather than the individual. The goal of the meeting is to deal with people's feelings and arrive at a solution that everyone can live with. User interfaces that deal with teleconferencing or remote meetings must look at meeting processes that are used in the target locale. Features such as voting must be evaluated for relevance. In addition, assumptions about acceptable meeting behavior must be examined. An interface that lets only one person "speak" at a time would be acceptable in the US, but users in southern Europe and the Middle East would grow very impatient about not letting everyone talk at once.

A tangible example of how rituals can influence the interface is shown in figure 7-4.

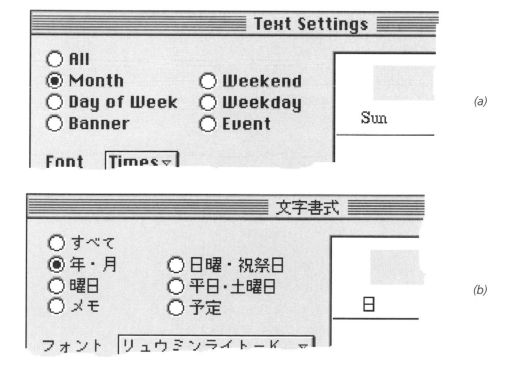

(a)

(b)

Figure 7-4 Calendar controls from ClarisImpact
Courtesy of Claris

Figure 7-4 (a) is a dialog box from the calendar feature of ClarisImpact. Note that "Weekend" is one of the selections. In the Japanese version, figure 7-4 (b), the notion of the weekend had to be changed to "Sunday" since Saturday can often be a work day.

Heroes

Heroes can be shared between cultures, but more often they are only relevant in a certain cultural context. They often represent an idea or are valued for their talent in one of the cultural rituals. Heroes can be both real and fictitious. Some heroes in the US include:

- **Superman** - Power, protector of the "American Way"
- **Martin Luther King** - Civil rights leader
- **Elenor Roosevelt** - Social activist, leader
- **Dwight Eisenhower** - Strong leadership
- **George Washington** - Father of the country
- **Amelia Earhart** - Courage, dedication, mystery
- **Thomas Jefferson** - Father of the Constitution
- **Abraham Lincoln** - Courage, statesmanship, honesty

When heroes or icons of this type are made into a software product, the chances for misinterpretation are great. For example, the product shown in figure 7-5 draws upon the image of Dwight Eisenhower and his presidential campaign motto "I like Ike." Overseas, this product would be out of context because its name would be meaningless, it could be offensive because of the appearance of a military figure, it is branded with the American flag, and it shows campaign pins that are part of the American presidential election process.

Figure 7-5 I Like Icon from Baseline
Courtesy of Baseline

Symbols

The last component, and also the one most prone to influence from other cultures, is symbols. Symbols are tempting to use in software because they can convey an idea with a simple word or image. Unfortunately, symbols and their interpretation can vary greatly. In particular, symbols can convey unintended negative messages. If symbols are used to try to convey a certain meaning in the user interface, there is a great chance that they will be misunderstood.

Respect other people's cultures in your design. You would demand the same. **!**

Common experience

Transcending the components of culture are common experiences that can often be a source that designers inadvertently draw upon.

History

Running through all of these components are historical issues. This includes traditional rituals, heroes from the past, and symbols of historical significance. "Historical" is a relative term. That is true both in a large country like the US as well as the rest of the world. In Boston, Massachusetts, figure 7-6 shows what is considered a historical building: the old state house. In California, it could be one of the Spanish missions, as shown in figure 7-7.

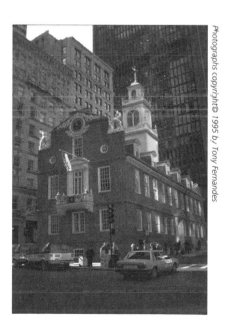

Figure 7-6 History in Boston   *Figure 7-7 History in California*

Photographs copyright© 1995 by Tony Fernandes

Figure 7-8 History in Europe

Courtesy of Shannon Halgrens

Figure 7-9 History in Japan

Would those pictures look historical to somebody who had the buildings shown in figure 7-8 or figure 7-9 next door? Who can say? Making assumptions about what is and isn't historical is tricky. Figure 7-10, which appears in ClipMedia 3 by Macromedia, is labeled "historic house." Historic to whom?

Figure 7-10 Whose history? Courtesy of Macromedia

Drawing upon historic events can be very prone to misunderstanding, and such references should be analyzed carefully relative to the target audience. The appearance of military figures can bring back some unwanted memories of a war-torn past. Some historical references can happen inadvertently. Sometimes, images can come perilously close to creating an undesired message. In figure 7-11, the packaging shows an image of a corporate professional cast in the role of a classic Hollywood director from the 30s implied by the megaphone. The other classic trapping of the stereotypical directors were knickerbocker pants and high leather boots. That outfit would be very reminiscent of the fascists in Europe during World War II. This packaging did a great job of suggesting a historic reference without using an image that could have been very negative.

Figure 7-11 Director packaging Courtesy of Macromedia

Geography and landmarks

Education within a locale teaches about the particular geography and landmarks that are most pertinent to the area. In fact, the whole perception of the world may change depending on where you are. World maps in the US tend to show the Americas in the middle of the map and therefore the world. Maps in Japan show Japan in the middle (Figure 7-12). In Scandinavia, the Scandinavian countries appear in the middle of the map and in their true proportions. Be aware of these differences when providing icons or images that show maps.

Photographs copyright© 1995 by Tony Fernandes

Figure 7-12 Japanese map

Certain geographic images are known worldwide such as the Nile River and the Amazon rainforest. This is true for landmarks as well. The pyramids of Egypt, the Eiffel tower in Paris (Figure 7-13), and the Taj Mahal in India are all well known and can be used to represent a country or locale. Aside from these very well-known images, relying on geography or landmarks to communicate an idea in a user interface can produce an attractive but meaningless image.

Photographs copyright© 1995 by Tony Fernandes

Figure 7-13 Eiffel Tower

Scientific theories

Although science is international and it uses international notations and conventions, curriculum regarding theories and terminology can vary. For example, some students in the world are taught that North and South America are one continent; others, that they are two. Of particular concern regarding this issue are multimedia titles whose content includes scientific topics. For example, Microsoft had to change its Dinosaurs CD-ROM when it went to certain countries in Europe because the theories on their extinction varied.

Catchy phrases and expressions

For a variety of reasons, people from a given locale often use a set of catchy phrases that are generally known by everyone. These phrases can be historic references or one liners that a famous comedian may have said many years back. The danger with these phrases lies in the designer's assumptions that they are internationally recognizable. The designer's culture has its own jingles and phrases and sometimes they are inadvertently used or punned. Below are some sources of catchy phrases that you should make sure do not influence your design. They are illustrated with examples from the US.

Advertising

Oh what a feeling, ...
The real thing.
Where's the beef?

Entertainment

Beam me up Scotty.
Take my wife, please.

Common

Neither rain nor snow...
Raining cats and dogs.

History

I have not yet begun to fight.
Don't shoot until you see the whites of their eyes.
We the people...

Symbols and Taboos

Symbolism is a major part of a culture's identity. The symbols can represent positive messages of national identity, good luck, and numerous other sentiments. They can also communicate very negative messages of death, bad luck, and threat. In addition, certain symbols denoting religious messages are almost always inappropriate.

To compound the problem, the same symbols may mean different things in different cultures. In addition, the same idea can be represented with different symbols in different cultures. Some symbols are very specific to a particular culture, and a rich familiarity with the target culture must be developed. For example, look at the image in figure 8-1(a) found at the entrance to a bathhouse in Japan.

Photographs copyright© 1995 by Tony Fernandes

(a)   (b)

Figure 8-1 Cutural symbols with varying interpretations

In it you see the drawing of a woman's head with a "no" symbol over it. In the background is a human figure. What does it mean? No women? No women on T-shirts? How about, no Mafia allowed? The Yakuza, the Japanese equivalent to the Mafia, wear tattoos all over their bodies. This sign is intended to give them the message that they are not welcome inside. How about figure 8-1(b)? You probably had an immediate reaction to it. In fact, it is a native American (Hopi) symbol that indicates the direction of the tribe's migration through the Americas. The same symbols can be found as a Japanese family crest as well as in many other cultures. It holds a different meaning in each one.

The human body can also be used to communicate any number of ideas; a creative expression is shown in figure 8-2.

Photographs copyright© 1995 by Tony Fernandes

Figure 8-2   Creative body language

! *Unless you understand the symbols and taboos of your target culture, you could be communicating messages with the user interface that are not intended.*

Design Rule 8: Remove taboos from the interface and use appropriate symbols

Because icons and images are used in most user interfaces, there is a danger that one or several of the images will be negative, insulting, or prone to misunderstanding. These types of symbols fall into the category of taboos. Taboos can be very visual in nature and therefore can inadvertently appear in a graphical user interface. These symbols should be avoided in icons, logos, sound effects, clipart, or any other kind of screen art.

Numbers

Numbers are glyphs that represent a quantity but they can also convey other meanings. For example, in the Western world, the numbers in table 8-1 are significant.

Number	Meaning
7	Lucky
13	Unlucky
69	Sexual connotation
666	Antichrist (religious)

Table 8-1 Western meanings for numbers

In Japan and other Pacific countries, a different set of numbers have meaning, as shown in table 8-2.

Number	Meaning
4	Death
7	Lucky
8	Future is better
9	Suffering

Table 8-2 Asian meanings for numbers

The reason that numbers 4 and 9 have the meanings they do is because they are homonyms for death and suffering, respectively. The number 8, when written, uses the same symbol as "the future is better." These numbers have a stronger impact than one might suspect. For example, in Hong Kong, tall buildings can be found that don't have any floors numbered 4. Others have lobbies on every fourth floor because nobody wants an office that is in any way associated with death. Likewise, license plates with the number 8 are a huge status symbol and are sometimes auctioned off to the highest bidder. If people will go to the point of having architecture respond to these symbols, what do you think the chances are the products shown in figures 8-3 and 8-4 will succeed in that part of world?

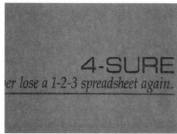

Figure 8-3 Superbase   *Figure 8-4 4-Sure(ly not)*

This doesn't suggest that certain numbers shouldn't be supported in the interface: You need to be able to type 4, for example. The point is that numbers that appear as a fixed part of the interface, say in a sample, should be picked very carefully to make sure they are appropriate for the culture of the target locales.

 The best way to find out about numbers is to ask people in the target locale. Don't count on people volunteering an objection during usability testing or market research.

The human body

The human body is a tremendous source of symbolism. Body positions, body parts, and gestures have been used to communicate for longer than recorded history. Many of these gestures developed independently of each other, and similar ideas are represented by a variety of symbols. In particular, it seems that the human body is a universally popular way to convey obscenities and insults.

Hands

Perhaps the richest gesture-based communication media are the hands. Figure 8-5 shows a common set of hand gestures used in the US. Can you associate a meaning with each one?

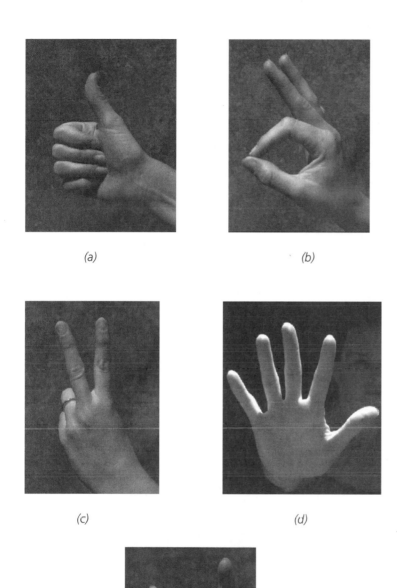

(a)

(b)

(c)

(d)

(e)

Figure 8-5 Hand gestures
Photographs copyright© 1995 by Tony
Fernandes

*Figure 8-5(b) also
signifies money in
Japan. Figure 8-6
signifies good luck in
Brazil.*

What if I told you that each of the gestures in figure 8-5 means the same thing to someone in another part of the world that figure 8-6 means in the US and some European countries? Surprised? It's true.

Photographs copyright© 1995 by Tony Fernandes

Figure 8-6 The finger

The thumbs up is an obscenity in Australia but only for older generations. Younger people have been influenced by US entertainment so much that they have adopted the US meaning and for them it is not an obscenity.

Figure 8-5(a) is used as the middle finger is in Australia; figure 8-5(b) is offensive in parts of South America; figure 8-5(c) is used as an insult in the UK; figure 8-5(d) is an insult in Greece, and figure 8-5(e) is an insult in Italy.

Some other versions of "the finger" are shown in figure 8-7.

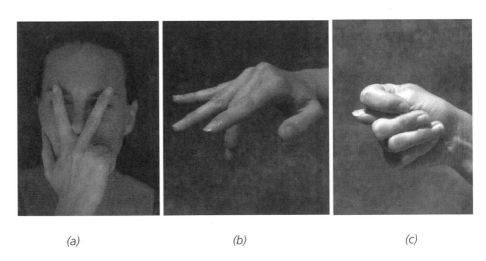

(a)   (b)   (c)

Figure 8-7 Some more creative fingers
Photographs copyright© 1995 by Tony Fernandes

Figure 8-7(a) is an obscenity in Saudi Arabia, figure 8-7(b) is the generic Arabic "finger," and figure 8-7(c) is the finger in Central America among other places.

In addition to insulting people, hands can be used for other purposes such as beckoning somebody. Although it seems like a standard notion, the way somebody is beckoned varies, as shown in figure 8-8.

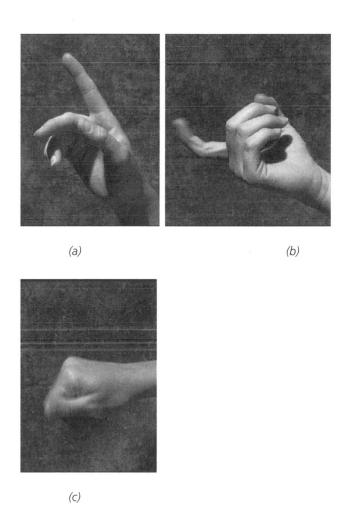

(a)   *(b)*

(c)

Figure 8-8 Beckoning gestures
Photographs copyright© 1995 by Tony Fernandes

Figure 8-8(a) is typically used in the US. Figure 8-8(b) is used in the US as well but in some parts of the world, it is only used to beckon prostitutes. Figure 8-8(c) is used to beckon in some parts of Latin America and Europe.

Another gesture that can be misinterpreted is shown in figure 8-9. To Americans, it could represent money if the fingertips are rubbed together. To Italians, it serves as a way of accentuating spoken words. In Portugal, it signifies fear.

Photographs copyright© 1995 by Tony Fernandes

Figure 8-9 Fear and money

Circling the nose, as shown in figure 8-10, indicates homosexuality in Colombia. By twisting it, you indicate that somebody is drunk. Note that the action is very similar to the motions for bad smells in the US.

Photographs copyright© 1995 by Tony Fernandes

Figure 8-10 Nose ring

As you can see, using hands in user interfaces is a tricky issue. But because hands can be so expressive, they can easily make their way into user interfaces. Like everything else, you must make sure that the gestures will not be insulting for your target locales. Figure 8-11 is just a sample of hand icons from several products. Note that some would be obscenities in some parts of the world.

Figure 8-11 Sample of hands in interfaces
Courtesy (clockwise from top left) Lotus, Microsoft, Apple, Davidson Software

Although hands are used for counting all over the world, the way people count is different. In the US, counting begins with the index finger and finishes with the thumb. In several European countries, counting begins with the thumb and finishes with the little finger. The Mac installer turns the cursor into a hand that counts in order to mark the passage of time. It counts the American way in all locales.

Even the way people count with their hands is an issue. You must understand how people do things in your target locale: There's no two ways about it.

The right and left hand can be significant. Certain parts of the world view the left hand as bad and evil. In some cultures, left-handed children have their left hands tied to their bodies so that they are forced to use their right hand instead. This bias to the right side has been around for a long time and has impacted many cultures throughout history. Expressions such as "right hand man" associate honor and significance with that side.

Alexander the Great defeated the Persian army by sending his best troops against the left side of his opponent's army, knowing that the other emperor's best troops would be on their leader's right. By taking advantage of this cultural trait, he was able to defeat a force much larger than his.

The head

In most countries, nodding left and right means no and up and down means yes. However, nodding up and down can mean no in diverse countries such as Bulgaria, Yugoslavia, and Turkey. Figure 8-12 shows two icons from the "Just Grandma and Me" CD-ROM from Living Books. The character nods its head to indicate no and yes, respectively. In certain parts of the world, the animation would be wrong.

Figure 8-12 No and yes controls from "Just Grandma and Me"
Courtesy of Broderbund

Feet

Feet are not quite as expressive as hands or the head, but they can be offensive or inappropriate. For example, feet on tables and chairs are offensive in countries such as Japan and Belgium. In Arabic countries, showing the bottoms of feet is very offensive: That part of the body is thought to be unclean. Like hands, the appearance of feet in icons, etc. may be inappropriate.

Other body parts

Disembodied body parts in general can also have meaning. Just the presence of the hand, an absence of a body or a leg or whatever, has meaning in Catholic Europe. This is because Catholicism has a richly embedded tradition in sacrifice. That is, if you want something, you have to be willing to sacrifice to get it. When people pray for things, they pledge a part of their bodies as a sacrifice. For example, "If my son gets better I will give up my left arm." When the son gets better and it's time to pay up, you don't chop off your left arm, instead you buy your left arm an effigy. In countries like Spain and Portugal, you can buy wax body parts that you turn in to the local cathedral. Figure 8-13 shows another type of sacrifice. In this case, it's young women's pony tails hanging at a cathedral in Evora, Portugal.

Kneeling positions can also vary in meaning. If a Westerner saw people with their heads on the floor, the observer might think they were very despondent. They may, in fact, be praying in an Arab country.

Photographs copyright© 1995 by Tony Fernandes

Figure 8-13 Sacrificed hair in Portugal

When it comes to body parts, just say no.

!

People and faces

When people communicate face to face, more than just words are exchanged. There are visual cues that suggest seriousness, social caste, status, and credibility. These are derived from clothing, facial expressions, and body language in general. In multimedia products or in any kind of anthropomorphic interface, careful attention must be paid to who is presenting what. Many societies have social castes that are relevant to the credibility of an individual. A small example of this is the derby, or bowler, hat in England. The use of this hat makes a social statement that the wearer is successful and is high ranking in business.

Of particular concern are instances of people or characters that are supposed to be humorous. Humor is certainly a notion that does not translate well. In American entertainment, you often see General Patton in parody to symbolize discipline and toughness. Somebody from another culture looking at that same parody will see a symbol of oppression, death, and colonialism; it will not be funny. Some people in the US can laugh at military characters because there hasn't been a war on US soil for over 100 years. That cannot be said for most of the world.

With more and more user interfaces becoming anthropomorphic, the risk of creating inappropriate material becomes greater. This is true not only because of the aforementioned body language issues. It is also true because status and other matters come into play: for example, what a person is wearing, the dialect they may speak, the color of their skin, etc. There is no such thing as a neutral person.

Figure 8-14(a) is supposed to represent a doctor but it also communicates white, male, middle age. Many messages are unconsciously communicated. When you look at the figure 8-14(b) from TaxCut, does "conservative, white, Western, male" come to mind? Is that a good guy or bad guy? When illustrations of people are used, there is a great chance that they may be inappropriate for every locale. Another way of dealing with this issue is to use characters and cartoons that are devoid of every physical characteristic. The faces in figure 8-15 from the Mac sharing control panel are devoid of any clothing and thereby are fairly neutral.

Some religious orders in Asia wear a similar headress to the one shown in figure 8-14 (a).

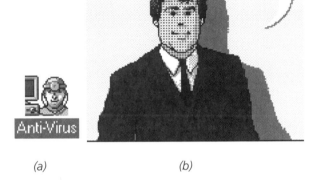

(a)   *(b)*

Figure 8-14 Real people in MS Windows and TaxCut
Courtesy of Microsoft and MECA Software

Figure 8-15 People in the Mac OS
Courtesy of Apple Computer

One can only image the difficulties Microsoft will have in translating the notion of Bob, the Microsoft social interface. It's already starting life with a very American name in a very American set of rooms.

If the interface presents people in video form or through animated sequences, proper greetings should be considered. For Western countries, a hello is sufficient. In Arabic countries, the motion for salam (touching the heart, forehead, and then continuing the motion past your head) would be appropriate. In Japan, a bow would be recommended. A bow is used not only in person, it is used in television shows that have a host such as the nightly news. It would be appropriate in software as well.

Certain facial expressions can be easily misinterpreted. For example, downturned eyes to most Americans mean that somebody is guilty or is weak. In countries like Japan, it signifies respect.

It's important not to stereotype the habits of people. The appearance of these stereotypes can communicate a lack of understanding about a culture. They can also be offensive. Just as people in the US are stereotyped as wearing cowboy hats, Bavarians are stereotyped as people that eat too much. Japanese people are stereotyped as all being short and carrying around cameras wherever they go. People in Africa don't all live in the jungle. People in Arabic countries don't all live in the desert. Everybody in France doesn't wear a beret. Everybody in Germany doesn't wear lederhosen. Unfortunately, the entertainment industry uses these stereotypes regularly, so don't let what you see in movies or TV make its way into your interface. Would you want people in another part of the world to design a product for the US based on the Dukes of Hazard? Be sure to portray people in a nonstereotypic manner.

If you use human figures, be prepared to change them for various locales.

!

Animals

Animals are significant on two fronts: one, they can have symbolic meaning; two, which animals are considered food varies. In the US, there are many meanings associated with animals. For example, a donkey and an elephant are used to indicate the Democratic and Republican parties respectively. A bear and a bull represent stock market trends. A black cat can be bad luck. A turkey represents Thanksgiving. The symbolism associated with animals varies all over the world. You must be very careful when including images of animals in your interface.

For example, cows have sacred meaning to the Hindu religion. That may explain why there was such a negative reaction to the moof by some people around the world. The drawing in figure 8-16(a) was used on the Mac mostly in the page setup dialog box. Some people were offended by it because it looked like it was half cow, half dog and therefore was treading on a sacred symbol.

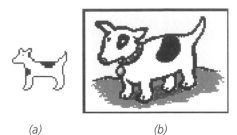

(a)   *(b)*

Figure 8-16 Apple moof and Powerpoint dog <small>Courtesy of Apple and Microsoft</small>

In another variation in figure 8-16(b), the animal's head is more doglike but the feet look like hooves. Make sure that your illustrations don't corrupt the image of an animal that may be symbolic.

Although pigs are considered dirty in some cultures, they can also be a symbol of good luck, as in Germany. Figure 8-17 shows a candy that is comprised of several German good luck signs: the pig, chimney sweep, four leaf clover, and mushroom.

Photographs copyright© 1995 by Tony Fernandes

Figure 8-17 German good luck symbols

In Japan, good luck is represented by the frog, in the US, it is a rabbit's severed foot. Somehow I like other countries symbols better.

Dogs are thought of as the lowest form of life in some cultures. In the Middle East, calling somebody a dog can be a powerful insult. This is also true in countries such as Spain and Portugal. Having the image of a dog on the computer screen as part of the interface would not be advised for those markets.

Snakes can have religious significance. For example, they are a symbol of the devil in the Judeo-Christian tradition. Other significant symbols are:
  • The owl is bad luck in India.

• The deer represents homosexuality in Brazil.

• The turtle represents long life in Japan.

In general, using animals as part of the interface can cause you problems internationally. Don't use them unless you have researched your locale well.

Animals can also represent time. The Chinese calendar uses animals to represent years. The animals also represent other traits. This is so true that abortions in China rise in years where the animal is viewed as having negative traits, and births explode in years where the traits are positive, such as the year of the dragon. Animals are serious stuff.

Be aware that even animal sounds are not international. For example, table 8-3 shows some of the sounds a dog makes all over the world.

Country	Sound
Denmark	vo vo
France	ouah ouah
Japan	wan wan
Portugal	beu beu
Germany	wow wow
US	bow wow

Table 8-3 Sounds of animals

Cats seem to say "meow" in most parts of the word except for Japan where they say "nyaan." Also, Japanese frogs go "gero gero" rather than "ribbit."

Food

Certain foods can be problematic. Shellfish, pork, and rabbits are all considered inedible by the Jewish religion. Since cows are sacred animals to some people, not everyone shares the notion that they represent food. To some people, the thought of eating a cow is as offensive as eating a dog is considered in the US. Of course, eating a dog would not be viewed as unusual in certain parts of Asia.

Other forms of food can also have meaning. Northern Telecom ran an ad in Japan with money bags full of peanuts to illustrate how cheap their product was. Unfortunately, peanuts are a symbol for bribery in Japan. The ad was pulled.

Plants

Plants such as the lotus plant have religious significance in several Pacific Rim countries. Carnations, often used at proms in the US, can signify death in other cultures.

Religion

Religion can be a very important part of a culture. One need go no further than the television to realize that religious differences are a significant enough issue that they can sometimes lead to violence. References to religion can therefore be uncomfortable at best. Religious symbols such as the Cross, Star of David, hands praying [figure 8-18 (a)], the menorah, the pentagram, the crescent, Buddha [figure 8-18(b)], etc. should never be used in a user interface. It's just pure TNT.

Photographs copyright© 1995 by Tony Fernandes

Figure 8-18(a) Hands praying

Courtesy of Shannon Halgrens

Figure 8-18(b) Buddha in Japan

An exception to this are religious symbols that have entered mainstream acceptance. For example, Santa Claus, which is associated with Christmas, is now more of a secular symbol for the holiday season. Santa Claus images can be found in just about every part of the world. Even in Japan, as the bags from a Japanese toy store in figure 8-19 illustrate, he is ubiquitous in December. This is why it makes sense for the clipart collection for Microsoft Works for Japan to include a Santa along with more traditional Japanese themes.

This bag has an interesting use of English.

Photographs copyright© 1995 by Tony Fernandes

Figure 8-19 Japanese bag

Photographs copyright© 1995 by Tony Fernandes

Figure 8-20 MicrosoftWorks clipart
Courtesy of Microsoft

Words

Words and abbreviations can carry unintended meanings. A spreadsheet with the abbreviation SS in the title would have negative connotations in Germany because of the dreaded storm troopers in WW II. Imagine a financial package that had a field for "IRA contributions" in England. Innocent words or abbreviations can have significance. This sort of thing happens all the time. As was mentioned in the introduction to this book, Mitsubishi originally introduced its Montero vehicle as the Pajero. Unfortunately, pajero is Spanish for masturbator and the Latin American market scoffed. There's a famous perfume called CoCo on the market. Co co is Portuguese slang for feces.

Even made up words and names can be problematic. Let's say you were putting together a CD-ROM game with some funny characters in it. Since you didn't want to use English names, you made some names up. You came up with Joda, Nabo, and Mona. These seemingly madeup names are all bad choices for use all over the world. Table 8-4 gives a sample of words that can trip you up in Spanish, Italian, and French-speaking markets.

Word	*Meaning*	*Language*
bollo	*vagina*	*Spanish*
bufo	*homosexual(derogatory)*	
goma	*condom*	
joda	*@#&%ed up*	
nabo	*penis*	
paja	*masturbate*	
pito	*penis*	
mona	*vagina*	*Italian*
sega	*masturbation*	
bite	*penis*	*French*
chat	*vagina*	
con	*vagina*	
pet	*flatulate*	
pine	*penis*	

Table 8-4 Bad words in nice languages

Believe me, you can spot profanity in your own language much more quickly than you can in others. As you can see from figure 8-20, unfortunate combinations of words can be created if you don't have a good understanding of a language's slang.

Photographs copyright© 1995 by Tony Fernandes

Figure 8-21 A Japanese store sign

If you make up any words, be sure to have somebody from the target locales read them over.

!

9 *Cultural Aesthetics*

Two things cannot be hidden: being astride a camel and being pregnant.
Lebanese

Have you ever gone somewhere and felt that it looked like some other place? Or been in a part of the world and noticed a building that looks like it's from another part of the world? Most people have. The reason is most people have internalized perceptions of what looks local and what looks foreign.

A user interface should always be striving to look familiar and friendly to its users. Chapter 6 discussed accomplishing this goal by portraying the correct everyday objects found in the environment. In this chapter, this technique is expanded upon by introducing the notions of cultural aesthetics.

Design Rule 9: Present the user with culturally appropriate aesthetics

If a product is being designed for a country or culture that you don't understand fully, effort must be put into piecing together a sense of what "looks right." The best place to begin is with history. One area in particular that is worth learning about is the history of design movements and their impact on your locale. Historical trends and styles have a continuing effect on the design found in various countries. Design movements have influenced artists, architects, and industrial designers . In turn, these influences make their way into the design of buildings, cars, consumer products, and objects that people see everyday. Therefore, they can be the foundation of a country's aesthetics.

There is a great deal of information about many design movements and their impact on certain parts of the world. Some of the classics include the Arts and Crafts movement, which was very influential in England, ultimately influencing Germany as well. Art Nouveau was enormously popular in Europe. As shown in figure 9-1, Art Nouveau forms made their way into architectural elements as well as consumer products such as champagne (figure 9-2). The Modern Movement, culminating in the Bauhaus, not only impacted Europe but most of the industrial world, including Japan. Its principles are found in the minimalist designs of German consumer products shown in figure 9-3.

Photographs copyright© 1995 by Tony Fernandes

Figure 9-1 Metro entrance in Paris

Photographs copyright© 1995 by Tony Fernandes

Figure 9-2 Art Nouveau in French products

Photographs copyright© 1995 by Tony Ferrandes

Figure 9-3 Bauhaus influence in German products

Many of these design movements are still influential today. Others have become pure history, although you often see them used to create nostalgic effects. Examples of design styles that have come and gone are "streamlining" which was popular during the 1930s and 1940s. During this period, everything from toasters to cars, as shown in figure 9-4, took on rounded shapes. Another is Art Deco which impacted the design of furniture, architecture, and of course American cinema marquees (figure 9-5). Companies such as Harley-Davidson motorcycles use these outdated design influences to create a sense of the past.

Photographs copyright© 1995 by Tony Fernandes

Figure 9-4 Streamlined design (1940s style)

Photographs copyright© 1995 by Tony Fernandes

Figure 9-5 Art Deco theater marquee

Some design movements are much more national[6] in nature. Italian design, with its use of bright colors and belief that form comes before function, has developed a very distinctive style. One of my favorite symbols of this type of design is shown in figure 9-6.

Figure 9-6 A Ferrari

Architecture, in particular, projects an unmistakable cultural look. For example, Greek revival architecture, figure 9-7, is common in Europe and the US. Intricate designs such as the gate in figure 9-18 are synonymous with Asia.

Figure 9-7 Capital building

Photographs copyright© 1995 by Tony Fernandes

Figure 9-8 Chinese gate

The ultimate goal of a user interface is to fade into the background. In order to accomplish this, the background must be understood and replicated on the screen. By understanding that shapes, colors, and texture influence a person's perception of location, a designer can tap into aesthetics that create a sense of place in the software.

! ***Learn about the influential design styles that affected the target locale. This information will give you a base of knowledge to draw upon as you start thinking about the visual designs for your target locale.***

Colors

Color can communicate function, quality, and nationality. It's a powerful part of human perception. This is why major corporations are willing to invest millions in using color to communicate their corporate values and identity. For example, when United Airlines changed from a domestic to an international carrier, they decided to communicate this fact with the color of the airplanes. The color change was supposed to communicate "international," "high quality," and "refinement." United wound up gravitating to a neutral gray with a rich dark blue. The gray was found to have no negative meanings in the countries they traveled to. In addition, it had the positive attribute of being considered a sophisticated color. The rich blue that was used for the bottom of the fuselage and the tail was intended to communicate luxury. As shown in figure 9-9, the difference in paint schemes is striking.

Photographs copyright© 1995 by Tony Fernandes

As you look at the two pictures, ask yourself which one you think would have a higher quality interior. Color talks!

Figure 9-9 United Airlines colors

Color can also connote function in certain countries. For example, orange is used for aid and emergencies on the highways of Switzerland. In Japan, green is used for the country's public telephones, as shown in figure 9-10.

Photographs copyright© 199= by Tony Fernandes

Figure 9-10 Color use on public devices

Particular countries also develop patters of color usage without any particular function. In some cases, color usage can be a nationalistic statement, as shown in figure 9-11. Colors can also be borne out of usage patterns. By tapping into these patters, color use can communicate a very specific message. For example, in the Netherlands, you can't help but notice the amount of blue (delft) that is used. It is used in the corporate identities of the country's major corporations, figures 9-12 and 9-13, as well as in everyday things such as taxi cabs (figure 9-14). When I asked people in the Netherlands about why objects such as the taxi cabs are blue, the response was "What other color would it be? Blue is the color of quality." In the case of the Netherlands, blue becomes a way of communicating quality.

Photographs copyright© 1995 by Tony Fernandes

Figure 9-11 Brazilian soccer fans

Photographs copyright© 1995 by Tony Fernandes

Figure 9-12 KLM Airlines

Photographs copyright© 1995 by Tony Fernandes

Figure 9-13 Philips blue identity

Photographs copyright© 1995 by Tony Fernandes

Figure 9-14 Dutch taxi

All this in turn affects people's taste. In figure 9-15, you can see the different cover designs of the same book for the Japanese and US markets. Clearly, there is a different take on aesthetics regarding what are considered "good colors" and what are not. By looking at the color usage in an environment, one can begin to piece together common patterns of usage and also recognize differences relative to your own taste. For example, in Japan, red and the pairing of red and blue are used a great deal in the environment as shown in figure 9-16. It's inescapable. Red often appears in buildings, etc., but it is also used quite a bit with text as shown in figure 9-17. In fact, a great deal of advertising uses text in red.

Figure 9-15 Japanese and American book covers

Figure 9-16 Blue and red together in Japan

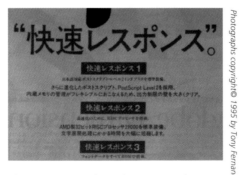

Figure 9-17 Red text is common in Japan

Software is just another part of this environment. When you look at Japanese software created in Japanese, as in figure 9-18, the same familiar colors begin to emerge.

Photographs copyright© 1995 by Tony Fernandes

Figure 9-18 Japanese software packaging

Don't get the impression that Japanese designers solely use bright colors, though. In fact, the majority of designs use very muted color schemes.

These observations can be combined to produce color palettes to be used when creating materials for a given culture. Three sample palettes are shown in figure 9-19(a-c) based purely on my observations of Japanese, German, and American designs. This is just a small sample of the color usage, but you can begin to see differences in the tone and varieties of color. Japanese design in particular uses a great

To get a good look at each color, cover the others so that you can only see one at a time.

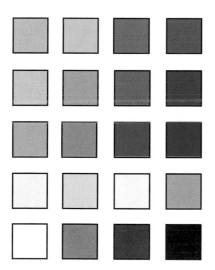

Figure 9-19(a) Japanese colors

deal of subtle color. German designs use a great deal of black, white, and grays.

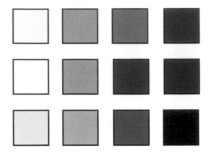

Figure 9-19(b) German colors

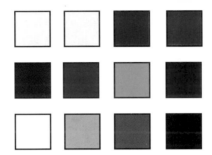

Figure 9-19(c) American colors

Recognizing these color differences is interesting, but what does it have to do with software? A great deal. Responding to these color differences is key to creating material that is appropriate for a locale. For example, figure 9-20 shows two calendar designs for ClarisImpact. Note the stark difference in color and style between the American and Japanese versions of the calendar.

The Japanese version of Microsoft for Windows J ships with a different set of clipart than the US version, figure 9-21. In the Japanese version, the color use and style of the art are exactly what you would expect as a Japanese user.

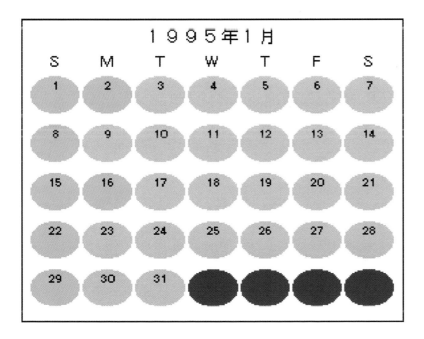

January 1995

Sun	Mon	Tue	Wed	Thu	Fri	Sat
1	2	3	4	5	6	7
8	9	10	11	12	13	14
15	16	17	18	19	20	21
22	23	24	25	26	27	28
29	30	31				

１９９５年1月

S	M	T	W	T	F	S
1	2	3	4	5	6	7
8	9	10	11	12	13	14
15	16	17	18	19	20	21
22	23	24	25	26	27	28
29	30	31				

Figure 9-20 American vs Japanese calendar styles from ClarisImpact Courtesy of Claris

Figure 9-21 Microsoft Works clipart Courtesy of Microsoft

Typography

Typography certainly embodies certain national and cultural elements and should be considered part of a locale's look. The significance of typography is evidenced by the policies of Nazi Germany. During the 1930s and 1940s, typeface use was dictated by law since the Nazis considered typefaces part of the German national identity. Today, typefaces are regularly used as part of corporate identities. Most people are not skilled in typography but, as with any cultural aesthetic, people know when they are being used incorrectly.

For example, do the examples of type in figure 9-22 seem appropriate to you?

EMERGENCY ROOM

Funeral Home

POLICE

The Bijou Theater

Old West Saloon

Figure 9-22 "Weird" typeface use

How about in Figure 9-23?

Emergency Room

Funeral Home

POLICE

THE BIJOU THEATER

OLD WEST SALOON

Figure 9-23 Familiar typeface use in the US

Remember that culture involves the programming of people in an environment. Because typefaces are all around, we have all been programmed in regards to their use. In the US, for example, there are a multitude of typefaces that are used for certain effects. For example, the sign in figure 9-24 is typical of signs dealing with motifs of the old American West. Figure 9-24, shows the use of the Bell Centennial typeface which can be found in almost all US telephone books. Figure 9-26 shows the use of the Copperplate typeface. It is a relatively trendy typeface that can be found in store signs and even wedding invitations. It's all part of the US environment.

Figure 9-24 Western typeface

Photographs copyright© 1995 by Tony Fernandes

Figure 9-25 Telephone book

Photographs copyright© 1995 by Tony Fernandes

Figure 9-26 Copperplate in action

As you might imagine, the appropriate use of typefaces varies all over the world. In particular, where US graphic artists tend to use serif fonts, European designers will use sans serif fonts. If you are not familiar with this terminology, figure 9-27 gives an example of each type. The serif fonts have extra ornamentation.

Figure 9-27 Serif and sans serif letters

Figure 9-28 shows text from the cover of a computer magazine, notice the serif fonts.

Figure 9-28 American typography

The same magazine in German shows a decidedly different choice of typefaces, as shown in figure 9-29. There are no serifs. This same difference can be found between many instances of German and US typographic taste.

Figure 9-29 European typography

Letter forms

In addition to certain typefaces contributing to the aesthetics of a place, typeface designs can convey a particular part of the world. For example, the typefaces in figure 9-30 have a distinct look that can immediately be associated with a country

Figure 9-30 Typefaces with national character

Typefaces are also often grouped into two categories: modern and traditional. This distinction seems reasonable enough but what users perceive as falling into these two categories varies. Figure 9-31 shows fonts that fit into the two categories from different parts of the world.

	Traditional	*Modern*
Japan	愛のあるユニーク	愛のあるユニーク
Germany	Aſsmannhauſen	Assmannhausen
US	The United States	THE UNITED STATES

Figure 9-31 Traditional and modern interpretations of text

A list of significant typefaces is shown in table 9-1.

Typeface	*Use*
DIN -(Mittel)Schrift	*European road signs*
Bell Centennial	*Telephone book*
Futura	*Germany in the twenties VW ads in the seventies, corporate America today.*
Caslon	*US and English books*
Lithos	*Trendy in the US friendly(ancient Greek inscriptions)*
Frutiger	*Designed for signage of Charles de Gaul Airport. Very popular in Europe*
Snell Roundhand	*Formal invitations in US*
VAG Rounded	*VW corporate font*
AGFA Rotis	*Trendy in Germany*
Heisei Mincho	*Traditional Japanese*

Table 9-1 Sample of typefaces used around the world

Influential geometry

In addition to design movements, you should become aware of shapes that have been historically significant and therefore influential. Shapes contribute to a sense of place because they can be found repeating themselves over and over again. Since they are part of the environment, people in that environment become ingrained with their presence. We are not dealing with innate ideas and tastes. More often, we are dealing with visual design traditions that have existed a very long time and that impact everyone that lives in an environment.

Architecture, graphic art, and industrial design are all influenced by geometric shapes that exist in the environment. For example, in the Western world, the golden rectangle has been very influential. It can easily be found in the entrances of buildings done in Greek revival architecture. In figure 9-32, it is the rectangle formed from the bottom of the triangle to the bottom of the columns.

Figure 9-32 Use of golden rectangle

The double square, which is the proportion of the tatami mat in Japan, is a very influential shape in Japan. Since every floor plan is designed to the proportions of a tatami mat, as shown in figure 9-33, it becomes an inescapable part of the environment.

Figure 9-33 Tatami mats

Circular and curved themes are also a big part of the Japanese environment. They are found in architecture as well as in printed form, as shown in figure 9-34.

Figure 9-34 Oval on a Japanese product

Other influences in the environment include the shape of the television screen, typical doorway proportions, etc.

Putting it all together

The interesting thing is that people in such an environment are not conscious of these shapes. It is such a normal part of the environment that it is not really thought about. Although users can't articulate what the right look is, they react when it is wrong. If you can't ask your users for this information, how do you get it? There are two options:

1. Hire a qualified design firm from the target locale. A graphic design or industrial design firm would be best.

2. Try to piece together the information yourself. You can get clues in architecture, graphic art, and industrial design. Together, those design endeavors represent many of the trends found in an environment. These influences should guide some of the decisions made in designing a user interface for a locale.

To illustrate the latter approach, I will use Germany and Japan as examples of how common shapes can be translated into the user interface. The goal will be to design splashscreens for a German and a Japanese product that convey a sense of tradition. This might be a design applicable for a business product with a conservative user base. A typical splash screen is shown in figure 9-35.

Figure 9-35 Typical splashscreen design Courtesy of Microsoft

Let's start with Germany. Clean layouts have been a hallmark of German design for hundreds of years. Grids play a very important part of many designs. These grids in turn create many straight lines and sharp angles. The net effect is a very rectangular and angular look to many designs. These rectangles and sharp angles can be found in architecture (figure 9-36), and in industrial design (figure 9-37).

Photographs copyright© 1995 by Tony Fernandes

Figure 9-36 German Architecture

Figure 9-37 German taillights

Photographs copyright© 1995 by Tony Fernandes

Given this fact, our splash screen certainly will be rectangular in nature. Given the color palette for Germany, the splash screen will have a black and white aesthetic. The typefaces used will be sans serif, as is the case with most high-quality designs in Germany. Additionally, the splashscreen will use image marketing techniques: it should show the type of person who will use the product rather than what it does. The layout will adhere to a rigid grid of rectangles. A sketch of all these elements together is shown in figure 9-38.

Tabellenkalkulation

Dieses Produkt wird Ihre Anforderungen erfüllen. Es ist unter strengsten Qualitätsnormen hergestellt mit großer Sorgfalt an Ihre Arbeitsbedingungen angepaßt worden.

Micro Gesellschaft

Figure 5-38 Conceptual German splashscreen

Japan

Japanese design is relatively formal. There are colors and shapes that are considered traditional. Of particular interest in Japan is the way circular shapes are used. They have historically been the shape for family crests, as shown in figure 9-39. Curvature can be found in everything from architecture as shown in figure 9-40 to corporate identities, shown in figure 9-41. Contrast the taillight design in figure 9-42 to the German ones. Circular references are certainly part of the environment. Of course, so are rectangles in the form of the tatami mat and other elements in the environment.

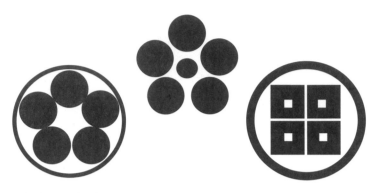

Figure 9-39 Japanese crests

Figure 9-40 A circle in Japanese architecture

Figure 9-41 Toyota and NTT logos
Photographs copyright© 1995 by Tony Fernandes

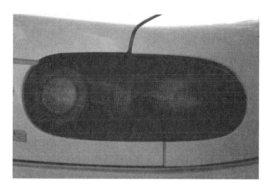

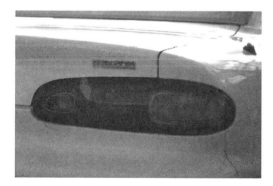

Figure 9-42 Japanese taillight design
Photographs copyright© 1995 by Tony Fernandes

To develop the design for the splashscreen, the shape comes first. Since the splash screen serves to identify the product, it draws upon round themes rather than rectangular ones. The strokes are traditional.

The colors used are muted and low key. The name of the product will be in red because of its importance in the grand scheme of things. Because a round area takes up a great deal of space, the inside of the circle will be filled in with a traditional pattern. The rectangle created in the middle will be the same proportion as a tatami mat. The completed design is shown in figure 9-43.

愛のあ

Figure 9-43 Conceptual Japanese splashscreen

On a more subtle level, recognize that the circle in the middle of a rectangular computer screen creates the subtle image of the Japanese flag.

By tapping into these indigenous shapes, a visual designer can create a certain feeling of familiarity: a feeling that is hard to quantify but nevertheless exists.

Cuteness

Since we are on the topic of Japan, one other aesthetic I'll mention is what I call Japanese cuteness. Where American clipart and imagery tend to be very professional, Japanese images tend to be very cartoon oriented, as shown in figure 9-44.

Figure 9-44 Cute designs

This style is acceptable enough in business that it finds its way onto business equipment. For example, the wait cursor in the Sony PalmTop device is a "cute" turtle that moves its head up and down and snores, as shown in figure 9-45. Many of the business clipart collections are in this style.

Figure 9-45 Sony Palmtop

Usability Testing

Usability testing is an absolutely necessary part of the user interface process. There are many companies out there that still don't test their products: I'll reserve comment. In the vast majority of the ones that do, there is a belief that once a product has been tested domestically, the results are valid all over the world. I hope that in reading the preceding chapters, you have come to the conclusion that there may be many unforeseen problems in the user interface because of national and cultural issues.

The desire to conduct usability testing and the opportunity to do so are very different things. On the surface, it seems like a daunting task whose funding might be difficult to justify. It can be done, however. This chapter presents a few words of wisdom based on the experiences of testing overseas by Lotus Development Corporation in Europe and Claris Corporation in Japan.

Words of wisdom

Here are some things to consider when putting a test together.

Location

If you have trouble
getting funding for a
test overseas, try
justifying it in terms of
its PR value to the local
sales office.

The first step is to pick the target locale. Once that is done, a suitable site in that locale must be found. Here are some criteria that you should consider when selecting the site:

- Pick a city in which you have a contact. If you are designing for a particular country, there have to be local sales or marketing people around or it won't sell.

- If you have a sales office in the country, consider using their facilities. You will not need to rent space and there will be help on hand.

- Pick a city that has an abundant number of target users.

- Make arrangements to stay close to the test site. After traveling a long distance, the last thing you want to do is spend time figuring out the local transportation system.

- Make sure the city you pick has a store nearby that sells things such as cables, plugs, and videotape. Also, make sure express delivery services are available in case something is left behind.

- Because of time differences, plan on using faxes and e-mails to do the bulk of your communicating with your test site.

Equipment

Discount usability methods, such as a pencil and paper, don't create any equipment issues. When more robust recording methods are used, its another story altogether. Below are issues to keep in mind as you set out.

- Decide what you will need: audio, video, logging software, etc.

- Call ahead to your test site and see what equipment is onsite. Make sure that the equipment is not only available, but is scheduled for your use. Keep in mind that equipment will have instructions and plugs described in another language. This is especially true in Japan. If you wind up using local equipment, make sure there is somebody there to help you set it up.

- If you bring your own equipment, use highly portable equipment. Portable usability labs are available on the market. If one is not available, you can put one together by connecting a video mixer to two video cameras and a VCR. Perhaps the simplest method is to use a camcorder with an external microphone. The immediate temptation is to just use equipment from the locale. Be aware that the world does not use the same video standard. The main standards are NTSL and PAL. NTSL is used in the Americas and Japan. PAL is used in Europe. If European equipment is used for a US audience, the tape produced will have to be converted.

- There are computer magazines and major companies around the world with testing facilities available for rent. In addition, universities may have appropriate facilities as well. Use your local contacts to investigate these possibilities.

- Make sure you have the right plugs and voltage converters. There's nothing like the smell of a $2000.00 camera burning to remind you that all electronic devices are not created equally.

- If work is being done in a country with a differing video format, consider taping in both simultaneously. This will allow you to leave with a tape, and the local office can keep a copy of the tests as well.

- If you are buying equipment for the test , make sure all of it is tested before you leave.

Recruiting

To conduct a test, you need users. In many cases, the target users speak a different language and therefore will have to be recruited by somebody else. Here are some tips for dealing with this issue.

- Develop criteria for the users you would like to test. Make sure the criteria are explained to whoever does the recruiting for you.

- If there are local salespeople, use them to recruit subjects based on the criteria you present them. They speak the native language and know the local companies and customers.

- If salespeople can't help you, consider hiring a local PR or marketing firm for the task. They are well suited for tracking down people and have excellent telephone skills.

Preparing

Like any endeavor, it takes preparation to succeed. Care must be given prior to leaving because traveling overseas is expensive and you will not have access to all your things.

- If a foreign language is involved, make sure you make arrangements to work with a translator. Ideally, you should train the translator in the fine art of testing. Since translators are not trained usability testers, they can often interfere by giving the user advice, thinking that they are being helpful. If the translator will meet you at the test site, allow enough time to go over the process before the first subject arrives.

- A task list should be developed and the test designed. You can write it in your native language and then have somebody translate it. It is very important that you go over the translation with the translator to make sure that the spirit of the questions and tasks has remained intact. Stress the importance of not taking liberties with the translation.

Scheduling

Make sure you allow plenty of time before the test for the following reasons:

- When you are settling on dates, take into account differing national holidays. This might effect not only how many people are willing to be subjects, but also your ability to make hotel reservations, etc.

- You will be jet lagged. You need to be sharp and rested to perform several days or weeks worth of testing. Take at least a day to get over the flight and another to do equipment/room setup.

- It will take time to explain exactly what you're doing to the people that are meeting you there. If you are doing the test at a local sales office, there is the additional burden of answering questions about what is going on at headquarters. Take this extra overhead time into account.

- Equipment needs to be set up and problems fixed. Quite often, things don't go 100% right and cables need to be bought at the last minute as well as dealing with equipment failures. Be ready for it and have contingency plans ready.

- Be prepared to work weekday nights and weekends. It is difficult for people to get time off from work in many countries.

Findings

Lotus in Europe

Lotus conducted a series of usability tests in Germany and Sweden. In one instance, the same test was given in the US and Germany. In the other, the test was only given in Germany. The tests were conducted at Lotus sales offices in those countries.

Prior to departing for Germany, a pilot test was run to make sure the test flowed and to get a sense of how long the process was going to take. Lotus used the local offices to recruit subjects. In particular, they wanted to make sure the target users spoke English to facilitate the interaction. The testing team consisted of one tester, a note taker with logging software, and a translator nearby.

Co-discovery (two users in the same room) techniques were found to work well. It was only problematic when one user's English was stronger than the other's.

Lotus learned that using English products in non-English countries did not affect the testing of new features. In fact, users were willing to talk aloud in English for note taking. In the first round of testing, they used a translated version of the product. In the second, an English version was used. Lotus's feeling was that both methods worked well. When they conducted testing on a translated product, they found problems unique to the particular language version. For example, in the German version of Lotus Freelance for Windows, the word "click" had been removed from the slide templates, as shown in figure 10-1, because the translators wanted to save space. Lotus had earlier found the word "click" to be very important to the usability of the product. Because this particular test was being conducted with the translated version, the problem was found.

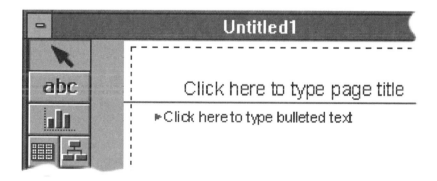

Figure 10-1 Lotus Freelance Courtesy of Lotus Development Corp.

In the Freelance test, Lotus also found that the slides their German customers wanted to create were black and white with a rectangular border. The original slide backgrounds were very colorful and dynamic.

The tests in Germany were videotaped in PAL and NTSC simultaneously. Usability testing in Europe is being conducted by a Lotus employee residing in Europe.

In general, the testing was found to be very valuable and produced some reactions that were different compared with the US users.

Claris in Japan

Claris conducted a usability test in Japan as part of the development process for one of its Japanese products. The test was conducted at Claris's Tokyo office.

Prior to leaving for Japan, three pilot tests were conducted: one in English and two in Japanese. Japanese-speaking users were recruited in the US to act as subjects. Since the translators were onsite, the English version served as a training exercise for the translators. The two Japanese pilots served as practice users to work out any remaining problems. Some video equipment was transported, but most was borrowed from the local sales office. This was facilitated by the fact that the video standard in Japan is the same as in the US: NTSC.

As a result of the pilots, several changes were made to the test script. Questions regarding "how comfortable" or how much they "like" the product were removed because they involved feeling and emotion which are issues that the Japanese are not accustomed to responding to.

The test in Japan was conducted with one tester and two translators. One translator conducted the actual test and the other translated for the English-speaking tester. A large monitor was placed in the back of the room where the tester and translator could observe without interfering with the test.

Claris learned a great deal about how cultural issues can impact testing overseas. In particular, Japanese protocol issues were adhered to. This included bowing when greeting somebody. It also included serving coffee or tea before business took place.

The users themselves created some issues not typically encountered in the US. For example, Japanese women spoke very softly. This put a huge premium on the quality of the microphone and where it was placed. Co-discovery techniques were used but they became problematic when people of differing status were put in the room together. In particular, women were found to talk very little when they were paired with a man. In a focus group setting, people were completely silent until introductions were made and the status hierarchy established.

Once the status issues were overcome, however, it was the Claris's opinion that the group settings worked best.

Like Lotus, Claris felt that they obtained many findings unique to the Japanese market.

Ergonomic standards

Talk of ergonomic standards has gone on for many years but in Europe, they are coming to life. In Germany, steps are being taken to make sure that software products live up to their promised ease of use. To that end, products are being tested for conformance to the ISO 9241 and the European directive for video display terminal work. Products that pass the usability test are awarded the seal shown in figure 10-2.

Figure 10-2 German usability sticker

The criteria used are not very specific. They include the following attributes for which products are tested:

- There will be no more than five user levels.

- Individual steps must be understandable and able to be visualized.

- Routine work must not demand a plethora of commands for its execution.

- The display background must offer a clear contrast to the text.

Soon, testing may become a necessity to enter markets overseas. In time, it may become a matter of law. No matter what, developing expertise in this area would be wise for all software companies that hope to compete internationally.

Business Justification

Whenever I speak on this topic, one question invariably comes up: Is it worth localizing a product from a business sense? There are plenty of arguments to be made on the humanitarian side. But alas, dollars and cents are at the heart of many managers' thoughts.

Other fields

The business issues discussed here only pertain to justifying localization.

When looking at other fields, most people don't question the fact that designing for the local audience is important. An example is food. If you are building a restaurant in a foreign country, you have to cater to local tastes even in the context of presenting your cuisine as ethnic food. When Pizza Hut opened restaurants in Japan, for example, they were determined to provide pizzas that catered to the local tastes of the Japanese. Some of their products were very unconventional by American standards: tuna and calamari pizzas. Their pizzas did well because they blended the American experience of eating pizza with the ingredients that local customers found tasty.

Architects adhere to the tastes and sensibilities of the people that live in a locale. Building a glass tower in the middle of conservative Beacon Hill in Boston would not be a worthwhile venture. Likewise, countries have their own architectural sensibilities and tastes. For example, Paris offers an interesting contrast of 19th century stone buildings, Art Nouveau decorations, and ultramodern designs. As architect, you wouldn't think of designing a building for Paris, figure 11-2 , in the style of American Colonial figure 11-1, though.

Graphic artists create work that adheres to tastes and sensibilities of their target audience. In the Lillehammer Olympics, the signage bore symbols that embodied Norwegian cultural and national sentiments.

Figure 11-1 A Colonial house in the US

Figure 11-2 The Louvre in Paris

When a consumer buys a product and it needs assembly, there is nothing more frustrating than receiving a set of instructions written in a language that he or she cannot understand. Providing directions in the native language is, at the very least, a statement of quality. The native language translation must be of high quality, however. In figure 11-3, directions from a Chinese toy create the sense that there may be some quality issues present by misspelling several words.

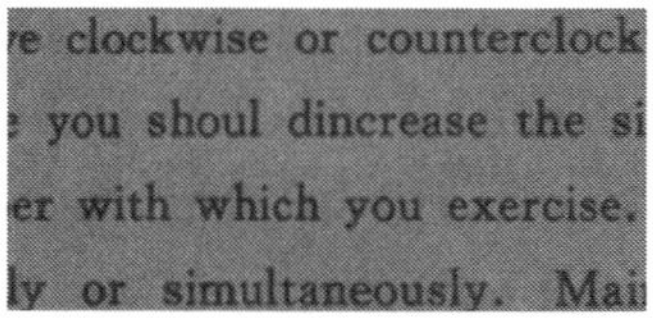
e clockwise or counterclock
you shoul dincrease the si
er with which you exercise.
ly or simultaneously. Mai

Figure 11-3 Directions from toy

Photographs copyright© 1995 by Tony Fernandes

Software companies, with rare exceptions, act as if no adjustments to their products are necessary. If a realization is made that changes are necessary, quite often localization is made a low priority. Often, localization efforts lack funding to make effective changes in the product and to maintain a high level of quality. In an informal survey I conducted of European computer press, their chief complaint about American software was the quality of the localizations.

Just a few short years ago, most American PC software was shipped overseas in English. When localized versions came along, so did a renewed competitive emphasis on changing the language. Now, more and more pressure is being put on the revenues coming from the international side of the business. Yet most software companies are thinking only of how they can economize on localizing, not how they can improve the products. Most large American software companies are reporting international revenues at around 50%. All this has created a vulnerable situation for those companies that are not willing to reexamine their process and priority in dealing with the issue of localization.

Given all this, here is my humble list of business issues that make high-quality localization and appropriate UI design an absolute necessity in the 1990s:

- Nobody would argue that usability is a significant factor in the success of a product. The usability of a product can vary greatly depending on the quality of the localized UI. In order to maintain a business edge, the product/interface design for the target nations must be considered right from the very beginning.

- As the software industry has found revenues overseas, so have other industries that use software products. Therefore, software that can handle multiple currency formats, have consistent file formats, etc. are becoming very valuable to large multinationals and smaller companies that are trying to compete internationally. With the new trade agreements and European Union, software that is savvy about how it handles international business is becoming increasingly important and marketable.

• Emerging countries are looking to invest in tools to make their industries productive and, therefore, competitive. As customers in these emerging countries evaluate products, they enter the process with no brand bias, compatibility issues, or previous investments in training. Companies search for the products that solve their problems and are of the highest quality for a reasonable price. If a product is not localized adequately, its perceived quality will suffer.

• It was once true that companies based purchasing decisions on the size of the companies that produced a product. Businesses have begun to find however, that it is now a battle of responsiveness and quality.

• By generating revenues from many parts of the world, a company can guard against being impacted by a recession in the domestic market or any one region of the world. A welllocalized product will aid in market penetration.

• In some cases, such as France, the correct support of the native language and keyboard conventions is mandated by law. If you don't have a product designed to work in France, you don't any sales in France, period.

• Consumer software products will gain greater acceptance if they are geared toward local tastes and aesthetics. In developed countries, such as Germany, the computers being bought for the home are high-end machines ready to jump into the multimedia revolution.

• By providing a well-localized and designed product for a foreign market, you will increase utilization of features leading to greater customer satisfaction.

• More and more software companies are starting up outside the US. By catering to local needs and tastes, they could begin eroding the market presence that most US software companies enjoy today.

Let's look at some case studies.

Customer satisfaction

A study done by the International Linguistics Foundation provides a good example of the impact that good localization can have on customer satisfaction. The study was done at a Brazilian-owned data processing company that was about to put its programmers through English classes because the IBM manual they used was not available in Portuguese. They interviewed 45 programmers. The results seemed to confirm that there was no was no need to localize the manuals. In general, the typical subject's opinion was "I can't speak English very well, but I can read the IBM manuals and perform the functions of my job." If this result had been arrived at through a marketing study, most likely no further work would have been done. In this case, reading comprehension testing was done anyway. The results were eye opening. Initial reading comprehension was only 15%. After a year of training in English, the comprehension was only up to 50%. You can imagine how limited these people were in using the products to their full extent. A competitor could come across as being more full featured merely by translating the material so that the programmers could understand it. In order for a product to stay competitive and provide customer satisfaction, it must be usable. Assumptions made regarding acceptance of English-language products in non-English speaking countries are dangerous at best. Everyone prefers to conduct their jobs in a language they understand well.

Local tastes and aesthetics

Claris Corporation has done an excellent job of designing products that cater to local needs. They enjoy a great market presence in Japan for instance, where they have several number one products on the Mac platform. The localized Japanese designs cater to both national and cultural issues. The changes start from the outside packaging and go all the way into the designs of the artwork that ships with the product. Figure 11-4 shows two of Claris's most succesful products as they look in the US and Japan. Claris's commitment to the local markets goes beyond the box and into the fucntionality of the products.

Figure 11-4 Claris products for US and Japan Courtesy of Claris

This focus on the demands of the local market has helped Claris achieve a 300% increase in Japanese sales over the last two years.

Dealing with multinational issues

Increasingly, there is a market for companies that can create international software solutions. One company that has capitalized on this is SAP of Germany. Their client-server product runs in 13 languages and has been praised for its handling of multiple currency formats, support for local regulations, and national taxation laws. Their product enables people to run companies with offices all over the world. What is the market for this type of product? Huge. Since 1990, SAP's revenues have grown from 400 million to 1.2 billion in 1994. BusinessWeek had a story about SAP in their August 8, 1994 edition that was entitled "America's Largest Software Success Story is German."

Homegrown products

In addition to SAP, there are many software products now being written outside the US. Because those software companies are exposed to localization issues from day one, they have an advantage over US software. In addition, local companies understand the needs of their customers intimately. For example, Japanese business tables are

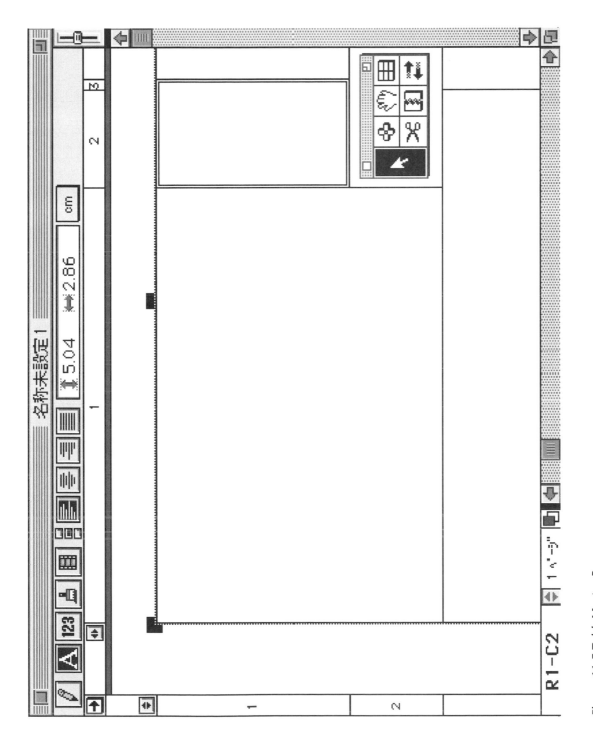

Figure 11-5 TableMaster Pro Courtesy of Catena

163

asymmetrical in nature unlike western conventions as shown in figure 11-6. Therefore, classic US spreadsheets are awkward to use for tables.

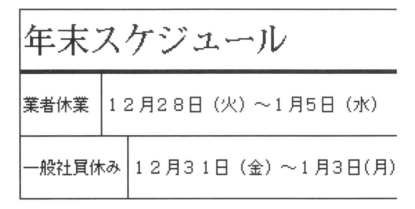

Figure 11-6 Japanese table

Because of these types of difficulties, products like TableMaster Pro, figure 11-5, from Catena of Japan have evolved. Its sole purpose is to make the creation of Japanese tables easy.

Quality localizations have also allowed products to enter the US market from other countries. Products that were developed in foreign countries that are popular in the US include Symantec's Q&A which was originally written in Germany. 4th Dimension, a popular Mac relational data base, was originally written in France. Some portions of the of 1-2-3 were acquired from a French software company. All these product have been successful in the US market. One of the reasons is that they bore no evidence of a foreign language or culture. This proves two important points.

1. Extremely well-localized software is doable and market success has followed.

2. Real hardcore products are being written and designed outside the US, and they are already successfully penetrating the market. If American software companies are unwilling to provide high-quality products, there will be plenty of opportunity for Japanese and European software giants to emerge. Let's not repeat the US automobile situation, shall we?

Invariably, somebody will point out that it would be financially impractical to localize designs for every single country. I agree with that. By the same token however, I argue that it MUST be done for the key markets of the product. The best way to approach the problem might be to concentrate on the large markets; those that yield 80% of the revenue. The countries that yield the largest markets will depend on your application.

The truth is that justifying localization from a business standpoint can be tough. There are so many factors involved in marketing a product overseas that you can attribute increased sales to any number of factors: increased marketing, buying cycles, you name it. The bottom line is that localizing a product properly is the right thing to do from both an ethical and a business standpoint.

Resources

This is a brief list of companies that provide services related to this topic.

ISO 9000 REGISTRATION AND TRAINING

KPMG Quality Registrar
150 John F. Kennedy Parkway
Short Hills, NJ 07078
Tel: (800) 716-5595

> Some companies require companies they buy from to be ISO 9000 certified. KPMG preassesses quality management systems to evaluate readiness of organization for registration, conducts registration assessment, follows up with periodic surveillance visits, and provides training to assist in enhancing quality management systems.

DOCUMENTATION

Terra Pacific
230 SW Third Street, Suite 302
Corvallis, OR 97333
Tel: (503) 754-6043

> Provides technical writing and editing, foreign language translation, brochures and newsletters, technical illustration and graphics, production and photography, consulting.

GECAP Gesellschaft für
Technische Information mbH
Inselkammerstraße 11
D-82008 Unterhaching
Tel: (+49-89) 61 41 77-0

> Coordinates and carries out all aspects of documentation
> localization, including editorial production, generation of
> graphics, formatting, proofreading, and supervision of printing
> and delivery.

International Language Engineering Corporation (ILE)
1600 Range Street
Boulder, CO 80301
Tel: (303) 447-2363

> Provides the production services needed to get product and
> support materials to distributor; desktop publishing, phototype-
> setting, camera-ready art, printing, packaging, disk duplication,
> assembly, warehousing, shipping. See entry under Software
> Translation.

SOFTWARE TRANSLATION

AT&T Business Translations
2400 Reynolds Road
Winston-Salem, NC 27106
Tel: (800) 633-6288

> Provides translation and localization of software and its accom-
> panying documentation to meet local requirements and cus-
> toms.

Berlitz Translation Services
257 Park Ave. South
New York, NY 10010
Tel: (800) 628-4808
(212) 777-7878

> Glossary development, document translation, software localiza-
> tion, desktop publishing and graphics services, project manage-
> ment, interpretation services, audio-visual and multimedia

services, consulting services, translatability and localization seminars.

Global Solutions, Inc.
44 Washington Street
Wellesley Hills, MA 02181-1801
Tel: (617) 431-2610

Provides translation, engineering, QA, desktop publishing, and design services.

IDOC, Inc.
10474 Santa Monica Blvd., Ste. 404
Los Angeles, CA 90025
Tel: (310) 446-4666
      (800) 336-9898

Offering the following services: translation, software localization, desktop publishing, internationalization, and multimedia.

ILE
1600 Range Stret
Boulder, CO 80301
Tel: (303) 447-2363

Documentation planning, manuals, software/tutorials, training/sales materials, quality assurance.

International Communications
One Apple Hill
Natick, MA 01760
Tel: (508) 651-9232

International Communications
18, rue de la Michodière
F-75002 Paris France
Tel: +33 (1) 42.66.59.60

Localization and quality assurance of software user interfaces, translation of software and hardware documentation, full electronic publishing services, product internationalization consulting services, localization of advertisements and marketing collateral, translation of multimedia materials.

Pan-American Access
P.O. Box 720006
Dallas, TX 75372-0006
Tel: (214) 824-4094

> Consulting services on the internationalization of products, translation, editing and proofreading of software and hardware documentation, localization of software and multimedia, product testing and quality assurance, localization of marketing and advertising materials, complete foreign language electronic publishing, audio and video translation, and product name analysis.

AUDIO VIDEO LANGUAGE SERVICES

Berlitz
257 Park Ave. South
New York, NY 10010
Tel: (800) 628-4808
     (212) 777-7878

> Providing voice-over replacement, lip sync (dubbing), UN-style narration, and subtitling. Also offers on-screen copy and graphics translation and replacement which complement the look and message of the original version. Visual special effects and moves are matched as closely as possible to maintain production value and uniformity. Music and/or sound effects are replaced or created as necessary.

MAGAZINES

Multilingual Computing
Email: info@multilingual.com

Multilingual computing is a great resource on this topic. It features timely articles as well as reviews of localized products. The advertising section is particularly handy for tracking down people who offer localization services.
Subscription: $55 per year.

Ease
Email: easemail@aol.com

Ease is an awesome newsletter covering the realities of designing user interfaces in the real world. It looks at the latest and greatest in recently released products. One section in particular covers international user interfaces. For the price of two software products, you get information and analysis on dozens.
Subscription: $395 per year.

TRAINING

Training based on the material in this book is available through Pedra Design which can be reached at (408)448-4724.

Code

Technical Issues

Although this book concentrates on design issues, no discussion of globalizing would be complete without mentioning some of the technical issues involved. The main issues are mentioned below as an aid in discussing these issues with developers and localization professionals. If you are responsible for designing world-ready versions, you have to make sure that these issues have been addressed. If they are not, there is very little that can be done to localize the product.

Development Rule 1:
Do not assume single-byte characters
One byte (8 bits) of information will allow you to represent 256 characters. The problem is that many languages, such as Japanese, require many more symbols. With 2 bytes (16 bits), you can represent 16,384 characters. If you write software assuming that characters will use only one byte, you will limit its ability to be localized enormously.

Development Rule 2:
Use driver settings from the operating system
Most operating systems are aware of what language they are running as well as particular formats for a given nation. This information typically resides in what is called a "country driver." The code should look at all appropriate formats in the country driver and represent them accordingly rather than make any assumptions about things such as time formats, date formats, units of measure, keyboard layout, etc.

Development Rule 3:
All text that appears to the user must be in external resources

When a modern GUI application is written, you can have all the text that appears originate from inside the code (hardcoded) or in files that live outside the main code (resource files). If text messages are hardcoded, it will be difficult to translate the product because it will be hard to find all the messages and it will also require that the product be recompiled. By placing all the text in a resource file, all the messages will be centrally located and much more easily changed via a resource editing tool. If nothing else is done to the code, this must be done in order to have any hope of localizing the language.

Development Rule 4:
Be careful of high ASCII

The ASCII characters are a set of characters used in many computer systems. Unfortunately, only the first part of the character table(low ASCII) is fixed. Latter parts of the table (high ASCII) vary from country driver to country driver. If engineers wants to use a character in the table, they can refer to it directly. Unfortunately, when the software is run on a computer using a different character driver, an entirely different symbol may appear. So for example, when programmers in Greece use an ASCII character that produces the ® symbol in the US, in they may get the Δ character.

Development Rule 5:
Don't make assumptions about fonts

Markets such as the Pacific Rim, the Middle East, and Eastern Europe have very different standard fonts. If the product as- sumes the existence of certain fonts used in the interface, the results will be unexpected.

Development Rule 6:
Don't hardcode physical space

Although abbreviations are acceptable in the US, they don't always make sense all over the world. If the product assumes that only a certain number of characters are needed to repre- sent an item, you can run into some big problems. For ex- ample, if a programmer hardcoded a calendar feature so that the representation of months was limited to the first three letters, in French, June and July would appear as Jui and Jui. This would be a problem.

Another place where this can have an effect is if a dialog box only allows enough space to show abbreviated English units or words. In many languages, words abbreviated and crammed into the space provided sometimes produces unacceptably cryptic controls.

Development Rule 7:
Beware concatenation

It is common in programming to construct strings on the fly in order to provide a meaningful phrase in relation to an event. For example, in most GUIs, the Undo command is the first entry in the Edit menu. Often, the command shown in the menu is Undo [last command]: verb-noun. This can be coded by starting a string with Undo and then concatenating the last command issued on the end. What happens, however, in a language where the verb appears after the noun, e.g., [last command] Undo? If the code makes the assumption that a phrase or sentence always contains a certain command in a certain location, you will have localizing problems.

Development Rule 8:
Avoid text in icons

With all the icons around, an interface designer may feel the need to contain text in order to be understood. Overlooking for a moment the fact that putting text in an icon defeats the whole purpose of having a clear image that people understand, the text is problematic because it can only be changed with a bitmap editor. Furthermore, the space is often so limited that English won't fit; never mind languages with long words like German and Finnish. The best solution is to provide on demand text similar to the way Balloon help works on the Macintosh.

Development Rule 9:
Change case properly

A trick to change the case of a letter is to use arithmetic. Given that the ASCII table is fixed, you can add or subtract an offset that will get back and forth from say A to a. Unfortunately, this type of operation makes the assumption that letters are represented in one byte. Many languages have their letters represented in two bytes. The arithmetic will not work correctly. The other assumption is that a written language has similar capitalization rules to English. Many languages, such as those of the Pacific Rim, have no such notion.

Development Rule 10:
Support mixed formats

The code must be written to allow error checking on a variety of address, measurement, time, and date formats. Additionally, it has to be able to deal with a variety of punctuation differences in numbers.

In terms of dealing with finances, assumptions about dealing with single currency symbols can be disastrous. Here's a scenario that was true in Lotus 1-2-3 a few years ago. If you wrote a spreadsheet in which you asked for a budget of $100,000 and sent it to Italy, the product would diligently follow Development Rule 2 and read format information from the country driver. With that information in hand, it would then display the number as L 100.000. Let me tell you that there's a world of difference between lira and dollars. What was needed in this case was a file format that supports a variety of currency formats regardless of the country driver being run. Support of multiple currency formats simultaneously is a necessity for multinational companies, global competitors, and banks.

Additionally, formulas that calculate financial information must be changeable as the product is shipped from country to country. Calculations, such as interest on loans, will vary.

Development Rule 11:
Keyboard commands cannot be hardcoded

As languages vary, so do the letters of the alphabet. This is true even in languages that use the Roman alphabet. For example, the Portuguese alphabet does not have a "Y" in it. Another problem with hardcoded keyboard commands is location. If you use keys in order to provide navigation, such as a game that might use "j" for left, "k" for right, "i" for up, and "m" for down on a QWERTY keyboard, you may find that those same letters may appear in different places on other keyboards.

Development Rule 12:
Sorting must be taken account

Sorting varies from country to country. Assumptions about what letter comes before what can be totally wrong. For example, in Spanish, "cho" comes after "co" because "ch" is treated as a separate character that comes after "c" in the alphabet.

Development Rule 13:
Allow for icons and other aesthetic components to be changed

In order for visual designs to be effective, they must provide the correct image of quality and appropriateness. Styles, content, and samples should not be hardcoded.

Development Rule 14:
Store product-specific text as tokens.

If text such as macro keywords will be seen by the user, it should be stored as token. Tokens are numerical representations of the words that reside in a table accessible by translators.

Development Rule 15:
Allow for text expansion in memory

When text is translated, it may expand in size. The code must be written so that larger text strings have adequate memory available. This is a problem if the code was written with static memory allocations.

Development Rule 16:
Get rid of unused resources

When many changes are made to a product, old unused resources get left in the product by mistake. Unused resources get in the way of translators. Remove all dialog boxes, icons, etc. that don't get used in the interface.

Development Rule 17:
Separate sound and voice

If you are developing a multimedia title, separate the sound from the voice. This will allow you to produce a universal music score or background sounds that can be mixed with voices in other languages.

Development Rule 18:
Support Unicode

Unicode is a standard intended to facilitate the use of characters from various scripts. By writing one interface to Unicode tables, the product will be able to use characters from just about all the scripts in the world.

Multimedia

Most of the issues discussed in this book regard the localization of text and visual imagery. Multimedia applications introduce the added complexity of sound, video, animation, and extremely rich content. Because of this, the skills you must assemble to produce a localized version of the multimedia title are quite different. They include:

- Voice-over artists
- Visual artists
- Film makers
- Domain experts
- Providers of local content

The following are some tips to keep in mind as you deal with localizing multimedia titles.

- Make sure that images are licensed for international use as well as for promotional use. When the product ships overseas, different laws will apply to it. This is of particular significance because of the amount of content in typical multimedia titles.

- Provide content that is relevant to the locale. If the product deals with geography, make sure that maps are changed.

- Keep text and background images in separate layers. Use tools that enable you to work this way. Products such as Photoshop allow you to put objects in multiple plains and then combine them to produce a final bitmap.

- Use scientific names for animals if possible. If more common names such as "tiger" or "dog" are used," be prepared to write them in every language you produce a product for. Also, be sure that you don't translate the name literally. For example a "yellow-bellied sapsucker" is not what the same bird would be called in other parts of the world.

- Put voice and background sound in separate files. For example, it is common to have music playing in the background as a voice narrates. Produce the music and voice recording separately and mix for each country.

- If the title contains scientific theories, be sure to have them reviewed by scientists in the target country. Assessments of the number of continents, how evolution came about, etc. have some interesting twists. Microsoft had to change its Dinosaurs CD-ROM when it shipped to some countries because the theory of how they became extinct varies.

- Use locally known cartoon characters and images. For example, cartoon characters such as Tin Tin, Asterix, and Lucky Luke are very popular in Europe. Hello Kitty is big in Japan.

D

References

1. Apple Computer, *Guide to Macintosh Software Localization,* Addison-Wesley, 1992

2. Euroclash, *ID Magazine,* January 1992, p. 61

3. De Mooij, Marieke and Keegan, Warren, *Advertising World-wide,* Prentice Hall, 1991

4. Hofstede, Geert as quoted by Marieke De Mooij and Warren Keegan, *Advertising Worldwide,* Prentice Hall, 1991

5. Tyler, Lyne, *Intercultural Interactions,* BYU 1979

6. Alderley-Williams, Hugh, *Nationalism and Globalism in Design,* Rizzoli International, 1992

Other material used

Axtell, Roger E., *Gestures: The Do's and Taboos of Body Language Around the World,* Wiley and Sons, 1991

Lunde, Ken, *Understanding Japanese Information Processing,* O'Reilly & Associates 1993

Tylor, Dave, *Global Software,* Springer-Verlag, 1992

O'Donnell, Sandra, *Programming for the World,* PTR Prentice Hall, 1994

Uren, Emmanuel, et al., *Software Internationalization and Localization,* Van Norstrand Reinhold, 1993

References

Kunitskaya-Peterson, Christina, *International Dictionary of Obscenities,* Scythian Books, 1981

Carroll, Rymonde, *Cultural Misunderstandings,* University of Chicago Press, 1987

Feldman, Reynold, *A World Treasury of Folk Wisdom,* Harper Collins 1992

E

Photo Credits

2-1 Tony Fernandes	6-21 Tony Fernandes
2-2 Tony Fernandes	6-24 Tony Fernandes
2-6 Tony Fernandes	6-25 Tony Fernandes
2-7 Tony Fernandes	6-26 Tony Fernandes
2-8 Tony Fernandes	7-1 Tony Fernandes
3-4 Lynn Shade	7-3 Tony Fernandes
3-12 Tony Fernandes	7-5 Tony Fernandes
3-13 Tony Fernandes	7-6 Tony Fernandes
3-29 Tony Fernandes	7-7 Tony Fernandes
4-1 Tony Fernandes	7-8 Tony Fernandes
4-2 Tony Fernandes	7-9 Shannon Halgren
4-3 Tony Fernandes	7-13 Tony Fernandes
4-4 Tony Fernandes	8-1(a) Lynn SHade
4-5 Tony Fernandes	8-1(b) Tony Fernandes
4-6 Bob Baxley	8-2 Tony Fernandes
4-7 Tony Fernandes	8-3 Tony Fernandes
4-8 Tony Fernandes	8-4 Tony Fernandes
4-9 Tony Fernandes	8-5 Tony Fernandes
4-13 Tony Fernandes	8-6 Tony Fernandes
4-14 Tony Fernandes	8-7 Tony Fernandes
6-1 Tony Fernandes	8-8 Tony Fernandes
6-2 Tony Fernandes	8-9 Tony Fernandes
6-3 Paul Fernandes	8-10 Tony Fernandes
6-4 Tony Fernandes	8-13 Tony Fernandes
6-8 Tony Fernandes	8-17 Tony Fernandes
6-9 Tony Fernandes	8-19(a) Tony Fernandes
6-10 Tony Fernandes	8-19(b) Shannon Halgren
6-11 Shannon Halgren	8-20 Tony Fernandes
6-13 Tony Fernandes	8-21 Shannon Halgren
6-14 Tony Fernandes	9-1 Tony Fernandes
6-17 Tony Fernandes	9-2 Tony Fernandes
6-18 Tony Fernandes	9-3 Tony Fernandes
6-19 Tony Fernandes	9-4 Tony Fernandes

9-5 Tony Fernandes
9-6 Tony Fernandes
9-7 Tony Fernandes
9-8 Tony Fernandes
9-9 Tony Fernandes
9-10 Tony Fernandes
9-11 Tony Fernandes
9-12 Tony Fernandes
9-13 Tony Fernandes
9-14 Tony Fernandes
9-15 Tony Fernandes
9-16 Shannon Halgren
9-17 Tony Fernandes
9-18 Tony Fernandes
9-21 Tony Fernandes
9-24 Tony Fernandes
9-25 Tony Fernandes
9-26 Tony Fernandes
9-28 Tony Fernandes
9-29 Tony Fernandes
9-32 Tony Fernandes
9-33 Tony Fernandes
9-34 Tony Fernandes
9-36 Tony Fernandes
9-37 Tony Fernandes
9-40 Tony Fernandes
9-41 Tony Fernandes
9-42 Tony Fernandes
9-44 Tony Fernandes
9-45 Tony Fernandes
11-1 Tony Fernandes
11-2 Tony Fernandes
11-3 Tony Fernandes
11-4 Tony Fernandes

All pictures attributed to Tony Fernandes are © Tony Fernandes 1995

INDEX